THE DARKER FACE OF THE EARTH

OTHER WORKS BY RITA DOVE

POETRY

Mother Love
W.W. Norton, 1995

Selected Poems
Pantheon / Vintage, 1993

Grace Notes
W.W. Norton, 1989

Thomas and Beulah
Carnegie-Mellon, 1986

Museum
Carnegie-Mellon, 1983

The Yellow House on the Corner
Carnegie-Mellon, 1980

FICTION

Through the Ivory Gate, a novel
Pantheon, 1992

Fifth Sunday, short stories
Callaloo Fiction Series, 1985

DRAMA

The Darker Face of the Earth, 1st edition
Story Line Press, 1994

"The Siberian Village," a one-act play
(in *Callaloo,* Vol. 14/2, 1991)

NON-FICTION

The Poet's World
The Library of Congress, 1995

THE DARKER FACE

OF THE EARTH

A PLAY

BY RITA DOVE

COMPLETELY REVISED SECOND EDITION

STORY LINE PRESS

1996

FIRST STAGE PRODUCTION:
Oregon Shakespeare Festival (OSF), Ashland, Oregon, July 27, 1996
with the support of a major grant from the W. Alton Jones Foundation,
and directed by Ricardo Khan.

All other performance and audiovisual rights are with the author. For production permission, contact in writing: Rita Dove, Department of English, Bryan Hall, University of Virginia, Charlottesville, VA 22903. For production and acting copies, contact the publisher.

Published by Story Line Press, Inc., Three Oaks Farm, PO Box 1108, Ashland, OR 97520-0052
Printed in the United States of America

This publication was made possible thanks in part to the generous support of the Nicholas Roerich Museum, the Andrew W. Mellon Foundation, the National Endowment for the Arts, US West Foundation and individual contributors.

LIBRARY OF CONGRESS CATALOGING-IN-PUBLICATION DATA
Dove, Rita.
    The darker face of the earth: a play / by Rita Dove.—Completely rev. 2nd ed.
p.   cm.
    ISBN 1-885266-19-7
    1. South Carolina—History—1775–1865—Drama. 2. Women plantation owners—South Carolina—Drama. 3. Mothers and sons—South Carolina—Drama.
4. Afro-Americans—South Carolina—Drama. 5. Slaves—South Carolina—Drama.
I. Title.
PS3554.0884D68   1996
812' .54—dc20   96-26121
                                                          CIP

ACKNOWLEDGMENTS

First and foremost I would like to thank my husband, Fred Viebahn, for his encouragement and help during all the stages of my work on the play—from the moment years ago in our sun-drenched apartment at Mishkenot Sha'ananim, Jerusalem, when I first told him my idea, through the many months the first draft spent relegated to the bottom of a drawer, to the day Story Line Press offered to publish the manuscript, and finally to the play's realization on stage. I am indebted to my daughter Aviva, who—in the clear wisdom of youth—never let her love for the play blind her to the wobbles and bloopers so unerringly detected by her laser eye.

I am also grateful to Robert McDowell of Story Line Press for his vision and enthusiasm and to Cynthia White, director of play development at Oregon Shakespeare Festival, for her unflagging support. Of the many people who have been involved in bringing the several renderings of this text to life I can mention only the principal players: Jennifer Nelson not only brought her inspired direction to a three week workshop at the Oregon Shakespeare Festival (my first behind-the-stage theatre experience), but directed staged readings of the first book edition at the Round House in Silver Springs, Maryland, and at the Roundabout Theatre (with Edgar Lansbury as producer) on Broadway; director Ricardo Khan's and dramaturg Sydné Mahone's passionate insights propelled the reading of an "interim" version at Crossroads Theatre in New Brunswick, New Jersey; and Derek Walcott directed a superb cast by lending his genius to a very poetic and dramatic reading of a version close to this one at the 92nd Street Y in New York City.

For my daughter

Aviva Chantal Tamu Dove-Viebahn

DIRECTIONS

The action takes place in antebellum South Carolina, on the Jennings Plantation and in its environs. Prologue: about 1820. Acts I and II: twenty years later.

The characters of Psyche and Diana, as well as the Doctor and Jones, can be played by the same actors, as long as it is made clear to the audience that they are different people. (Both the Doctor and Psyche, who only appear in the prologue, are older than Jones and Diana, who only appear in the later scenes: The Doctor is in his fifties, while Jones is in his thirties; Psyche is in her mid-teens, while Diana is about twelve years old.)

On occasion, the slaves comment upon the play somewhat in the manner of a Greek chorus. Individual characters are bound by time and circumstance; the chorus of slaves is more detached and omnipresent. By moving and speaking in a ritualized manner, they provide vocal and percussive counterpoint to the action. The slave woman who occasionally steps forward as the narrator, is quietly present in all slave scenes.

C A S T

Female slaves:
> PHEBE
> PSYCHE
> SCYLLA (pronounced "Skilla")
> TICEY, a house slave
> DIANA, a young girl
> SLAVE WOMAN/NARRATOR

Male slaves:
> HECTOR, an African
> ALEXANDER
> SCIPIO (pronounced "Sippio")
> AUGUSTUS NEWCASTLE, a mulatto

The whites:
> AMALIA JENNINGS LAFARGE
> LOUIS LAFARGE, Amalia's husband
> DOCTOR
> JONES, the overseer

The black conspirators:
> LEADER
> BENJAMIN SKEENE
> HENRY BLAKE

Other slaves and conspirators

P R O L O G U E

T H E B I G H O U S E :
porch; Amalia's bedroom; Louis's study; hallway

(HECTOR, a slave in his early twenties, is standing on the porch, look-ing up at a second story window. PHEBE, a slave girl in her early teens, runs onstage; she is coming from the basement kitchen. Skinny and electric, she is chuckling to herself.)

PHEBE

What some people won't do
for attention! Shore,
he's alright-looking—
but that ain't qualification enough
for the big white bed
in the big white house!

(laughs at her own wit; then, skipping in a circle, sings)

Stepped on a pin, the pin bent,
and that's the way the story went!

PSYCHE

(offstage)

Phebe! Phebe! You up there?

PHEBE

Here I am, Psyche!

(PSYCHE enters. She is petite, shy; though not much older than Phebe, she treats her like a little sister.)

13

PSYCHE	You shouldn't go running off by yourself, child.
PHEBE	Look: Hector on the porch.
	(She giggles and points to HECTOR.)
PSYCHE	Leave him be, poor soul.
PHEBE	Aw, Psyche! Anybody crazy enough to be standing there, thinking he—
PSYCHE	Shush now, chile!
	(PHEBE shrugs, hums and skips again. The other slaves straggle in, tired from the day's work, whispering among themselves, a suppressed excitement in their manner.)
PHEBE	What took you all so long? Slower than a pack of lame turtles.
ALEXANDER	*(a dignified man in his forties)*
	We all ain't quite so spry as you, gal.
PHEBE	Shh!
	(Everyone freezes.)
	I thought I heard something.

14

PSYCHE	Aw, girl—
SCYLLA	*(a tall dark woman in her twenties)*
	Must be a hard birthin'.
PSYCHE	I sure hope she make it. Her mama—
SCYLLA	Her mama was the weakest excuse for a woman ever dropped on this earth. But this one—
	(with a significant look to the window)
	this one got her daddy in her.
ALEXANDER	Nothing but trouble, I tell you. Nothing but trouble.
	(Lights up on AMALIA's bedroom... AMALIA JENNINGS LAFARGE lies in a canopy bed, a thickly swaddled babe in her arms. She is an attractive white woman, close to 20 years old, who exhibits more intelligence and backbone than is generally credited to a southern belle. The DOCTOR, an older whiskered gentleman, is pacing the floor. AMALIA, though exhausted, appears amused.)
AMALIA	Well, Doctor, isn't he beautiful?
DOCTOR	This is serious, Amalia! If the niggers get wind of this—

(AMALIA begins humming a lullaby to the baby.)

AMALIA

Don't get melodramatic, Doctor;
You'll frighten my son. See?

(Baby raises a cry; AMALIA continues to hum while the DOCTOR keeps pacing. Among the slaves, SCYLLA stands up, clutching her stomach.)

SCYLLA

Oh! Oh!

OTHERS

What is it, Scylla? What is it?

SCYLLA

It's out in the world.

(The slaves look at her in fear.)

ALEXANDER

Lord have mercy.

(During the ensuing scene in the Big House, the slaves gather around Scylla as she tries to straighten up but cannot; slightly hunched, she goes over to HECTOR, whose gaze is still fixed on the window.)

(AMALIA's husband rushes into the bedroom. LOUIS LAFARGE is a handsome man in his twenties. The DOCTOR holds him back.)

LOUIS

Doctor—

DOCTOR

Everything's fine. Just go on back outside.

LOUIS	Can't a man see his own child?
	(tears himself free and rushes over to the bed)
AMALIA	What, Louis—struck dumb?
LOUIS	My God!
AMALIA	Isn't he a fine strapping boy?
DOCTOR	This is unnatural.
LOUIS	Who did this to you? I'll have him whipped to a pulp—
AMALIA	*(hissing)* So it's all right for you to stroll out by the cabins any fine night you please? Ha— the Big White Hunter with his scrawny whip!
LOUIS	That tears it!
DOCTOR	Quiet! They might hear.
LOUIS	I'll kill her!
	(LOUIS lunges at AMALIA; the DOCTOR restrains him.)
DOCTOR	Hold it, sir! Calm yourself!

AMALIA	*(to the DOCTOR)*
	Daddy tried to keep me from
	marrying him—but I was in love
	with riding boots and the smell
	of shaving cream and bourbon.
	I was in love with a cavalryman
	and nothing could stop me,
	not even Daddy!
	(to LOUIS, who is being forced into an
	armchair by the DOCTOR)
	But not even Daddy
	suspected where you would seek
	your satisfaction.
	It was your right
	to pull on those riding boots
	and stalk little slave girls.
	God knows what you do to them
	in the name of ownership.
	(Depleted from the bravado she has mustered,
	AMALIA bends over the baby so they won't
	see her exhaustion. LOUIS, still sitting in the
	armchair, grabs the DOCTOR by the shirt and
	pulls him down to his level.)
LOUIS	Get rid of it! Kill the bastard!
DOCTOR	My charge is to preserve life,
	Mr. LaFarge, not to destroy it.

LOUIS	What's the matter? Aren't you a man?
DOCTOR	(scathingly; then a fierce whisper)
	My manhood isn't the question here. Do you want your business smeared across the whole county? Think for a minute: What have we got here? A fresh slave. New property. And you're in need of a little spare change, aren't you? I understand the cards haven't been much in your favor lately.
LOUIS	What are you trying to say, Doctor?
AMALIA	Stop your whispering, gentlemen. No one's going to touch this baby!
LOUIS	You can be sure I'll never touch you again!
AMALIA	That's one blessing.
DOCTOR	Is this baby worth destroying your life?
	(pulling LOUIS aside)
	Give me a minute alone with her. I'll make her see reason. Go on, now.
	(The DOCTOR shoves the reluctant LOUIS out of the door, then moves quickly to the window

to peek out on the slaves below. PSYCHE sees the curtains move and shushes PHEBE, who has been skipping in little circles from excitement. HECTOR and SCYLLA are in the shadows of the porch, invisible from the window. The DOCTOR returns to AMALIA, who is singing to the baby.)

DOCTOR

You can cease your motherly blandishments, Amalia. He's gone.

AMALIA

I knew you were good for something besides tonics and botched surgeries, Doctor!

DOCTOR

Oh, you're mighty clever, Miss Jennings—
no wonder your marriage is a disappointment.
Hell, your Daddy saw it coming;
he worried about you. How many times
did he have to haul you back from the fields,
kicking and scratching like a she-cat?

AMALIA

And just who was I supposed to
play with—the pigs and the chickens?
Daddy could run a plantation
but he didn't know the first thing
about raising a daughter. All morning
he'd teach me to calculate inventory,
but he expected his slippers darned come evening!
And when I refused, off I went—
to finishing school and the Charleston
society balls.

	(Lights up on LOUIS, sitting on the bed in his room, head in hands.)
LOUIS	Spare change. Spare change! How they all smirk! I know what they're thinking. "Louis sure slipped into a silk-lined purse!" *(takes a swig from a flask in his jacket)* Damn his blasted Hippocratic oath! *(paces, agitated; then stops, an idea dawning)* That's it! Of course. Doctor, I'll save you the trouble. *(He rummages in drawers; lights up on AMALIA's room.)*
AMALIA	When I came home from Charleston with my brand new dashing husband, Daddy had the slaves line the path from the gate to the front porch; and as we walked through the ranks each one stepped up with the nosegays they had picked— awkward bunches of wildflowers. I was laughing, gathering up bouquets and tossing them to Louis. We were almost to the porch when suddenly there appeared this . . . this rose. One red rose,

AMALIA (con't.)	thrust right into the path so we had to stop. I recognized him right away. We hadn't seen each other since Daddy sent him to the fields. We used to sneak out to Mama's old cutting garden; it was overgrown and the roses had run particularly wild! *(softly, remembering)* One day he covered me in rose petals, then blew them off, one by one. He'd never seen anything like them back in Africa. *(in wonder)* And there he stood, all grown up, with one red rose held out like it was a piece of him growing straight from his fist. "What a lovely tribute to the bride!" I said— *(shaking off the spell of the memory)* then passed it to Louis to tuck in with the rest.
DOCTOR	I suppose there's no sense in talking about your duty to the institution of marriage.

AMALIA	I made one mistake—Louis. I don't have to go on living it.
DOCTOR	Oh, there's where you're wrong, Amalia Jennings. Some mistakes don't right themselves that easy. Some mistakes you live with until you die. *(Lights up on LOUIS in his bedroom as he emerges from the back of the wardrobe with a pair of spurs, still trailing red ribbons)*
LOUIS	*(sneering)* There they are! Amalia's Christmas present— fancy new riding spurs! Won't they make a special "christening" present for the little bitty baby to tuck in with its blanket! *(LOUIS chuckles as he pockets the spurs and leaves the room; lights up on AMALIA and DOCTOR.)*
DOCTOR	How long do you think it will take before your slaves begin to speak back? To botch the work and fall ill with mysterious ailments? Then who will help you—Louis? An overseer who knows his mistress

DOCTOR (con't.)	is tainted with slave funk? In a bad year, how much will you have to beg to get a tab at the store? Who will you invite to tea, Amalia— your dashing blackamoor?
AMALIA	What a convenient morality, Doctor.
DOCTOR	I'm just trying to save your Daddy's good name. As for your precious little bundle— how long do you think he'll last with Louis feeling as he does? How long before your child accidentally drowns or stumbles under a horse's hooves? You can't keep him, Amalia; if you truly love him, you cannot keep him.
	(AMALIA buries her face in the pillow and begins to weep.)
DOCTOR	I know a family who handles these . . . delicate matters. They'll raise him and arrange for sale when it's time.
	(AMALIA clutches the baby to her.)
	He'll be treated well. I'll make sure of that.

(Silence. AMALIA stares at the baby.)

AMALIA   Give me a little more time!

DOCTOR   You had nine months.

(The baby makes a noise; she lays him on her breast.)

AMALIA   There's no way back, is there?

(A knock at the door.)

DOCTOR   There he is. Now:
I'll take the baby to Charleston tonight.
You must play the wronged wife.
No matter the truth—whatever the truth—
this affair was an act of revenge,
your retaliation to Louis's philandering.
But you won't keep the child
to taunt him, oh, no! Instead,
you'll forgive and forget . . . and show him
how to turn a profit besides.

(AMALIA stares at the DOCTOR with disgust. The DOCTOR opens the door.)

Come in, sir.

(LOUIS enters, glaring.)

This is a damned tricky situation,
but I think I've sorted it out.

DOCTOR (con't.)	(warming up to his role as the arbiter of respon-sibility and morality; pacing self-importantly)
	Out of rage and sorrow over your philandering behavior, Louis, Amalia has responded in kind. An extreme vindication, true, and utterly reprehensible—unless we remember what prompted it in the first place. Are we agreed?
	(Both LOUIS and AMALIA are silent.)
	As for the bastard child . . .
	(pauses for effect)
	Amalia has agreed to let it go. I have a friend in Charleston who likes raising slaves from the ground up. He's familiar with the story of the distraught wife confronted with the evidence of a husband's wandering lust.
LOUIS	No! I won't take the blame!
DOCTOR	No one need know it's come from the Jennings Plantation.
LOUIS	What about the niggers? They're out on the lawn, waiting for news.

DOCTOR	We'll say the poor soul expired directly after birth, took one breath and died. I've taken the body away.
LOUIS	No funeral? Niggers love funerals.
DOCTOR	No—Amalia didn't want a funeral. They'll believe it. They have no choice. *(to AMALIA)* You better make sure the father keeps his mouth shut.
AMALIA	*(haunted)* Who would believe him?
LOUIS	I must say, your ingenuity is impressive, Doctor. It's what I'd call a "master" plan. *(pointing to the sideboard where AMALIA keeps an oblong wicker sewing basket, trimmed with red velvet rosettes and lined in blue silk)* That basket—surely you'd donate your sewing basket to the cause, Amalia? It would fit so nicely behind the good doctor's saddle.
DOCTOR	*(examines the basket)*

DOCTOR (con't.)	Yes, that will do.
	(LOUIS places the basket next to the bed.)
AMALIA	Go tell them. Spread the sad tidings.
	(She says this with difficulty. DOCTOR and LOUIS exit as AMALIA carefully unwraps the baby and inspects him, top to toe. Lights up on the DOCTOR and LOUIS in the hall; TICEY, a house slave in her forties, approaches them.)
TICEY	How's Miss Jennings, suh? The baby sure sounds like a big one!
DOCTOR	*(harshly)* The baby's dead.
TICEY	Dead? But I heard it cry!
DOCTOR	He cried out once. Poor little thing had no more breath left.
TICEY	Now if that ain't the strangest thing . . .
LOUIS	*(sharply)* What's so strange about it? The baby just up and died. Happens all the time.

DOCTOR	Look at you, standing here arguing like a fool hen, while your mistress is in there crying her eyes out! *(shaking his head)* Now go on out to those niggers— I know you got them waiting by the porch. Tell them there'll be no wailing <div align="right">and moaning,</div>no singing or mighty sorry, Ma'am. Miss Jennings wants no funeral. Miss Jennings wants to forget. Go on now, scat!
TICEY	Yassuh. Sorry suh. *(TICEY exits. During the following scene she approaches PSYCHE, takes her aside, whispering. At PSYCHE's shocked reaction, the slaves, except for HECTOR and SCYLLA, crowd around. TICEY retreats back into the house while the other slaves lower their heads, softly humming in a frozen tableau. HECTOR falls to his knees; SCYLLA stands over him, severely bent.)* *(In the bedroom, AMALIA embraces the baby one last time.)*
AMALIA	This basket will be your cradle now. Blue silk for my prince, and a canopy <div align="right">of roses!</div>Don't be afraid: It's warm inside.

AMALIA (con't.)   *(places first a small blanket, then the baby in-*
                   side, takes one last look, nearly breaking down)

                   I dreamed you before you came;
                   now I must remember you before you go.

                   (collects herself as she wraps the blanket around
                   the baby and closes the lid)

DOCTOR   Let's get this over with.

LOUIS   Go ahead. Doctor, I—I'll wait here.

                   (The DOCTOR enters the bedroom.)

DOCTOR   Ready?

                   (AMALIA averts her head, thrusts the basket
                   at him.)

                   I wasn't sure you had it in you,
                   but I'll say one thing, Amalia Jennings—
                   you are your father's daughter.

                   (DOCTOR exits with the basket. AMALIA buries
                   her face in the pillows.)

DOCTOR   I best be on my way.

LOUIS   You have a hard ride ahead of you, Doctor.
                   Would you care for a bit of bourbon
                   to warm your way?

DOCTOR	*(slightly surprised)*
	Why yes, that would do nicely. Just put it with my things
	(As the DOCTOR turns to get his coat and hat, LOUIS slips the spurs in the sewing basket, under the blanket, then puts the flask into the DOCTOR's bag.)
LOUIS	There, you're all set— best medicine made by man!
DOCTOR	It's over, Louis. Nothing left but to forget.
LOUIS	Have a pleasant journey, Doctor.
DOCTOR	I will try.
	(Lights go out as the DOCTOR exits. The SLAVE WOMAN/NARRATOR steps forward. During the NARRATOR's speech, the SLAVES go about their tasks, humming as the lights slowly warm to sunrise and the stage begins to transmogrify, simulating the passing of twenty years: a tree growing, the big house being enlarged, etc.)
NARRATOR	Take a little seed, put it in the ground; the seed takes root, sends its tendrils down

till the sapling shoots
its branches high—
roots piercing ground,
limbs touching sky.

Now the mighty tree
is twenty years tall;
seed become king,
and the king takes all.

ACT I
SCENE ONE

THE COTTON FIELDS

(DIANA, a slave girl, collapses. SCIPIO, a young slave working nearby, hesitates.)

SCIPIO

Move it gal, or
you'll feel it later!

PHEBE

(helping her up)

Lift in your knees, Diana;
try not to think about your blood.
Tomorrow's Sunday—
tomorrow you can rest.

DIANA

(derisively)

Blessed be the Sabbath!

PHEBE

The child's too young to tote that sack.
She should be helping in the kitchen,
like we was raised.

ALEXANDER

You was raised with Massa Jennings,
Phebe—and he been gone these
                              twenty-some years.
You know his daughter got other ideas.

PHEBE

She grow eviller year for year.

ALEXANDER	Ain't right, a woman running a plantation like that.
SCIPIO	Woman? She's more man than woman.
PHEBE	And more devil than man.
ALEXANDER	Ever since she lost that child.
PHEBE	Oh, Alexander!
ALEXANDER	White folks feel a loss as much as we do— it's just that they ain't used to losing. I tell you, Miss Amalia went crazy in the head the day she lost that baby boy.
SCYLLA	That's not the way Ticey told it. (SCYLLA is severely bent over and walks with a limp. Her gaze is fearful.)
ALEXANDER	(to DIANA) Nowadays old Ticey don't tell us field niggers nothing. But that night she come from the big house and say to Psyche . . .
PHEBE	That's enough, Alexander.

DIANA	Phebe, what was my mama like?
PHEBE	Chile, you heard that story a hundred times. Ain't no different now, just 'cause you turned to a woman yourself.
DIANA	Please, Phebe.
PHEBE	(tenderly, as she resumes picking cotton) Psyche was the sister I never had. Why, she pulled me offa trouble so many times, I thought her hand had growed to my shoulder!
DIANA	(begins to cry) I wish I'd a known her.
PHEBE	Childbirth can kill the strongest woman.
ALEXANDER	Or kill the child.
SCYLLA	You still believe the white folks? That baby weren't born dead. Ticey heard it cry. I seen the doctor carry it off in a basket, but it weren't dead. I felt it kick.
DIANA	(wiping her tears) The baby kicked?

35

ALEXANDER	Scylla got her powers that night.
SCYLLA	(staring at DIANA, who shrinks back)
	The child was born alive! I know. I felt it.
PHEBE	Scylla . . .
SCYLLA	The veil was snatched from my eyes— and over the hill I saw bad times a-coming. Bad times coming over the hill on mighty horses, horses snorting as they galloped through slave cabin and pillared mansion, horses whinnying as they trampled everything in their path. Like a thin black net the curse settled over the land.
DIANA	What curse?
PHEBE	Don't pay her no mind.
SCYLLA	The curse touched four people.
DIANA	(getting scared)
	Who were they? Who were the four people?
SLAVES	Black woman, black man, white woman, white man.

SCYLLA	When the curse came I stood up to meet it, and it knocked me to the ground.
SLAVES	Black woman.
SCYLLA	My womb dried up, but the power churned in me.
PHEBE	We best get back to pickin'. No tellin' where Jones got off to—
SCIPIO	Same place he always "gets off to"— that clump of timothy at the spring where he's tucked his whiskey!
	(SCYLLA appears to be in a trance; SLAVES accompany her in a syncopated whisper.)
SCYLLA	Hector, son of Africa— stolen from his father's hut, sold on the auction block!
SLAVES	Black man.
SCYLLA	Hector was a slave in the fields until Miss Amalia took him up to the house. He followed her like her own right shoe. When she felt faint, he brought her iced lemon water; when she started to show,

SCYLLA (con't.) he helped her up the stairs;
when the baby kicked,
he soothed her.
But when her time came
he had to stand out by the porch
like the rest of us.
And when Ticey brought the news
Hector fell to his knees
and ate dirt like a worm.
Now he lives alone
and catches snakes in the swamp.

SLAVES Black woman, black man—
both were twisted
when the curse came over the hill.

SCYLLA While the slave turned to grief,
the master turned to business.
Miss Amalia hiked up her skirts
and pulled on man's boots.

SLAVES White woman.

SCYLLA And Massa Louis . . . Massa Louis
took off his riding breeches—

SLAVES White man.

SCYLLA —and shut himself upstairs.
Some nights you can see him out
on the balcony, staring at the sky:
He has machines to measure the stars.

SLAVES	Black woman, black man; white woman, white man!
SCYLLA	Four people touched by the curse: but the curse is not complete.
DIANA	I'm scared.
PHEBE	*(in spite of herself)* Did you have to tell her so much, Scylla? She's just a child.
SCYLLA	She's old enough to know. And you're old enough to know better.
PHEBE	I was there, too. I didn't see no horses comin' over the hill. You just crumpled up like a leaf. *(AMALIA enters unseen in riding clothes, whip in hand.)*
SCYLLA	I can strike you down like lightning, Phebe. I can send demons mightier—
AMALIA	What's this?
PHEBE	How—how de do, Miss Amalia! We was just trying to figure out what to do with Diana here.
AMALIA	She seems healthy enough to me— good stock, young and fresh.

PHEBE	*(motioning for DIANA to look sicker)*
	She fell out something awful. It don't look like she feel too good—
AMALIA	You aren't here to play doctor, Phebe. Where is that Jones? Jones!
	(JONES is nowhere to be seen. Impatient, AMALIA prods DIANA with the whip stock.)
	Lazy pack! I swear I've seen cows smarter than you! Jones!
JONES	*(rushes in, wiping his mouth with his sleeve)*
	Yes, Miss Jennings?
AMALIA	Get these niggers in line! Drink on your own time.
JONES	Yes'm.
AMALIA	I'll see you this evening up at the house.
JONES	Yes, Ma'am. I'll be there, Ma'am!
	(She strides off; JONES mops his brow with a huge handkerchief.)
	Goddamn niggers, gotta watch you every second!

Get that gal back on her feet!

(cracking his whip)

Keep your mouths shut and your hands picking
or you'll feel my lash, sick or not!

(watches them resume work; then exits)

SCYLLA   I believe it's about time for you
to pay me a little visit, Phebe.
Tomorrow evening—
after the moon's set.

PHEBE   Aw, Scylla, I didn't mean nothing—

SCYLLA   It'll be pitch dark. Take care
you don't trip on the way.

(BLACKOUT.)

A C T   I
S C E N E   T W O

T H E   B I G   H O U S E :
parlor; Louis's study

(LOUIS is visible at the window of his study, peering through a telescope at the stars; he occasionally takes notes or sips his brandy.)

(AMALIA sits at the desk in the parlor; JONES stands.)

JONES	Sorry about this afternoon, Ma'am. That little gal seemed real sick, you know.
AMALIA	Mr. Jones, I am aware you come fresh from the well-groomed slave holdings of Dawson's Plantation. And I was not so naive, upon hiring you, to believe Dawson's high-minded economic philosophy had not rubbed off on you. But that's not what I called you for. I bought a new buck yesterday: here are his papers.
JONES	*(glancing through the documents)* Miss Jennings! You can't be serious!
AMALIA	Something wrong, Jones?
JONES	Augustus Newcastle? That slave's the most talked-about nigger along the southern seaboard!

AMALIA	Good! We'll be famous.
JONES	Story goes he belonged to a British sea captain who treated him like his own son, and promised him his freedom when he died. But the brother who executed the estate sold the boy to pay off the debts. After that, the nigger went wild. They lost count of how many times he ran off, how many times they caught him— *(frantically leafs through the papers)* Here it is: "Twenty-two acts of aggression and rebellion." Twenty-two separate acts!
AMALIA	That's why I got him so cheaply.
JONES	But Miss Jennings! They say his back's so laced with scars it's as rutted as a country road. Rumor has it he can read and write. If you don't mind my saying so, Ma'am, an educated nigger brings nothing but trouble. Sure as I'm standing here, he'll stir up the others.
AMALIA	I wonder just how smart he is.
JONES	It's a miracle no one ever killed him.

AMALIA	*(sharply)*
	I own Augustus Newcastle, and I'll make him serve up. Any objections?
JONES	No, Ma'am. Sorry, Ma'am.
AMALIA	They're bringing him over tonight; put him in the barn and chain him down. You can show him around tomorrow. If he's as smart as they say, he could help you oversee the ginning. You may go.
	(This last is a jab at JONES, who looks at her for a moment, then turns on his heel and exits.)
	(BLACKOUT.)

ACT I
SCENE THREE

IN THE FIELDS

(Sunday. The slaves have been "let out in the fields" to occupy them-selves as they please. They have settled into two groups—some joke, tell stories, and dance, while others are quieter, chanting and praying. As the lights come up, the groups are rivaling each other in melody, the quieter ones humming in minor key while the others counterpoint in a jauntier tune.)

SCIPIO	Have you seen the new man? Mister Jones been showing him around.
ALEXANDER	I saw 'em down by the gin house. That's one wild nigger.
PHEBE	He spent last night chained in the barn. Chained!
SCIPIO	Must be mighty tough. Heard tell he's sailed the seas!
DIANA	Did he sail the seas to Canada? *(Shocked silence; everybody looks at her.)*
ALEXANDER	Gal, don't let nobody hear you say that word; Miss Amalia'll have your head on a stick.

ALEXANDER
(con't.)

As far as you concerned,
there's nothing in this world
but South Carolina and this here plantation.

(AUGUSTUS enters in leg chains, followed
by a watchful JONES. AUGUSTUS is a tall,
handsome young man with caramel-toned skin
and piercing eyes. His righteous anger is thinly
concealed behind his slave mannerisms. JONES
bluffs his way with a squeaky bravado.)

JONES

Here's the new buck you all
been whispering about!

(removes the leg chains; then, to AUGUSTUS)

You're lucky it's Sunday. Tomorrow
you'll get a taste of how things run
around here. First horn at day-clean!

(JONES exits. There is a moment's awkward
silence as AUGUSTUS rubs his ankles where
the chains have chafed. He looks up, calmly surveying
the two groups.)

SCIPIO

Welcome, stranger, welcome.
They call me Scipio.
What do you go by?

AUGUSTUS

Augustus.

SCIPIO

(stretching the name out, trying to make it fit
his tongue)

	Au-gus-tus? Ain't never heard that one before. What kind of name is that?
AUGUSTUS	The name of a king.
	(Uneasy silence.)
PHEBE	Don't pay Scipio no mind. He's always joking. I'm Phebe. And this is Alexander.
	(ALEXANDER nods, warily.)
	Alexander been here longer than anyone, I reckon.
ALEXANDER	How do.
	(SCYLLA enters with the water gourd and watches the introductions with a hard eye. PHEBE rushes to introduce them.)
PHEBE	And this here's Scylla. Scylla, he's the new one, go by the name of—
AUGUSTUS	Augustus Newcastle.
SCYLLA	Newcastle. Is that your captain's name?
AUGUSTUS	Scylla was the rock, Charybdis the whirlpool, that pulled the sailors down.

(General astonishment.)

PHEBE

Now this little girl—

(pushes DIANA over to AUGUSTUS)

was born and raised
right here on this plantation.

AUGUSTUS

What's your name, child?

DIANA

(shyly)

Diana.

AUGUSTUS

My, my. The sun and the moon
all in one morning!

(The slaves look bewildered. He laughs softly.)

Don't mind me. I'm just glad to meet
you all.

(Some SLAVES take up their chant again. AUGUSTUS walks upstage and stands looking into the distance. Although they are curious, the other SLAVES let him be. Only DIANA stares after him.)

PHEBE

Come on, Scipio, give us a story.

SCIPIO

You always wanting a story!
How many stories you think I got?

PHEBE	I think you grow them in your sleep.
SCIPIO	Well, I ain't got a story this time.
PHEBE	Aw, Scipio! You dog!
SCIPIO	But I got a song:

(accompanies himself on a handmade string instrument while his friends clap, pat their bodies, etc.)

The possum said: don't hurt me,
I'm harmless if you please!
The nigger said: I'm harmless, too,
And got down on his knees.

The possum cocked his little head
And contemplated long;
You're running just like me, he said
And joined into the song.

(Laughter. DIANA walks over to AUGUSTUS.)

DIANA	What you looking at?
AUGUSTUS	Just looking.
DIANA	Ain't nothing out there but the swamp.
AUGUSTUS	Do you know what's beyond that swamp?
DIANA	What?

AUGUSTUS	The world.
PHEBE	*(to SCIPIO)* Is that all?
SCIPIO	No, there's more: *(singing)* That night the nigger had himself A pot of possum stew. That harmless meat is just the thing To warm your innards through!
DIANA	What did you mean by the sun and the moon?
AUGUSTUS	Beg pardon?
DIANA	The sun and the moon—you asked my name and then you said you had the sun and the moon all in one day.
AUGUSTUS	You're a curious one, aren't you? Well—a long time ago there were gods to look after the earth and the sky. Phoebus was the god of the sun; your friend's name is Phebe. And your name stood for the moon. People wrote poems to Diana, goddess of the moon.

DIANA	What's poems?
AUGUSTUS	A poem is . . .
	(looking over at SCIPIO)
	. . . a song without music.
	(looks off towards the swamp)
	Who's that old man?
DIANA	Phebe, Hector's coming up from the swamp!
PHEBE	Don't fret, chile. Hector talk kind of crazy sometimes, but he don't hurt nobody.
AUGUSTUS	His name is Hector?
PHEBE	Yeah. Massa Jennings give it to him straight off the boat. He used to talk African—but he forgot most of it.
AUGUSTUS	What does he do in the swamp?
PHEBE	*(catching a warning look from SCYLLA)*
	He lives there.
AUGUSTUS	Hector, mighty warrior, abandoned by the gods.

DIANA	You know a lot of things.
AUGUSTUS	Nothing you couldn't learn if you had the chance.
	(Enter HECTOR, now middle-aged, dressed in muddy rags. He appears more African than in the first scene. He carries a dead snake in a net and looks around with wild, piercing eyes, then wanders up to DIANA.)
HECTOR	*(tenderly)* Eshu Elewa ogo gbogbo! *(DIANA shrinks back. HECTOR taps AUGUSTUS on the shoulder, holding out the net.)* I catch snakes: big ones, little ones. I'm going to catch all the snakes in the swamp.
AUGUSTUS	I don't know much about snakes, my friend.
HECTOR	I'm gonna catch all the snakes in the swamp! They grow and grow, so many of them. But I'll kill them! I'll kill them all!
SCYLLA	Sshh, Hector! Don't let the snakes hear! *(She puts her arm around HECTOR and pats him gently on the back, all the while staring at AUGUSTUS, as the lights dim and go out.)*

ACT I
SCENE FOUR

SCYLLA'S CABIN;
OUTSIDE OF THE SLAVE CABINS

(Night. SCYLLA sits behind a crude table strewn with an assortment of bones, twisted roots, beads, and dried corn cobs. Three squat candles light up her face from below. In the distance can be heard the rhythmic ecstasy of the Sunday night "shout." PHEBE at the door with a small cloth bundle. She looks behind her, knocks.)

SCYLLA	Come in, child. Sit.
	(PHEBE sits.)
	I know your heart, Phebe. You have made the spirits angry!
PHEBE	I never meant no harm—
SCYLLA	Shh!
	(picks out a forked branch and arranges the candles in a half circle around the branch)
	The body moves through the world.
	(places a round white stone in the fork of the branch)
	The mind rests in the body.
	(sprinkles green powder from a vial onto branch and stone)

SCYLLA (con't.)	The soul is bright as a jewel, lighter than air. *(blows the powder away; the candles flare, PHEBE coughs)* There is a curse on the land. The net draws closer. What have you brought?
PHEBE	Here! *(shoves her bundle across the table. SCYLLA pulls out a pink ribbon and drapes it over the branch)*
SCYLLA	"Eshu Elewa ogo gbogbo . . . *(sprinkling powder on the first candle)* . . . oki kosi eyo!" *(The candle flares and goes out.)* You have tried to make the earth give up her dead.
PHEBE	Oh!
SCYLLA	*(pulling out a shell necklace, draping it over the branch)*

"kosi eyo,
kosi iku . . .

(*sprinkling powder on the second candle*)

. . . kosi ano!"

(*The second candle goes out.*)

PHEBE   Have mercy. . .

SCYLLA   You have tried to snatch words
back from the air. The wind is angry.
It will take more than these—

(*indicating PHEBE's offerings*)

to satisfy him.

PHEBE   (*pulls a white handkerchief out of her pocket*)

Here's . . . a hankie from my mama.
There's a little lace on it—see?

(*SCYLLA snatches the handkerchief, places it on the branch and repeats the procedure with powder and incantation.*)

SCYLLA   "Ni oru ko mi gbogbo
omonile fu kuikuo
modupue—
baba mi Elewa!"

SCYLLA (con't.)	*(The third candle flickers but stays lit.)*
	Ah!
PHEBE	What is it?
SCYLLA	Are you prepared to hear what the spirits have to say?
PHEBE	*(gathering courage)*
	If there's something I need to know, I want to know it.
SCYLLA	I give you two warnings. First: Guard your footsteps; they are your mark on the earth. If a sharp stone or piece of glass falls into the path you have walked, you will go lame. Second: Guard your breath; do not throw with words. Whenever the wind blows, if your mouth is open, your soul could be snatched away. That is all.
PHEBE	Scylla . . .
SCYLLA	Go now!
	(SCYLLA mutters over the candles as PHEBE hurries off, shuffling her feet to blur her footprints as she flees. On the way she passes

*AUGUSTUS, who is squatting outside a cabin.
He is in ankle chains. In the distance the slaves
can be heard humming during the "shout".)*

AUGUSTUS   Evening.

PHEBE   *(caught in the act of obliterating her steps;
embarrassed)*

Evening.

AUGUSTUS   Back from the shout?

PHEBE   *(trying not to speak)*

Uh-uh.

AUGUSTUS   What's your hurry? Why don't
you keep me company for a spell?
Unless you're scared of me, that is.

PHEBE   Scared of you? Why should
I be scared of you?

AUGUSTUS   I can't think of a reason in the world.
Come on, rest yourself.

(PHEBE sits down beside him carefully.)

AUGUSTUS   Sure is a fine night.

(PHEBE nods.)

AUGUSTUS (con't.)	You're trembling.
PHEBE	I am?
	(claps her hand over her mouth)
AUGUSTUS	And I don't believe it's entirely my doing.
	(He says this in a mildly flirtatious manner, then looks off, unaware of the effect this has on PHEBE, who has stopped thinking about Scylla and is now acutely aware of AUGUSTUS as a man. AUGUSTUS continues speaking, preoccupied once again with his hatred.)
	Fear! Fear eats out the heart. It'll cause kings and field niggers alike to crawl in their own piss. Listen to them sing! What kind of god preaches such misery?
	(gesturing in the direction of the "shout")
	White-fearing niggers. Death-fearing slaves.
PHEBE	Ain't you ever scared?
AUGUSTUS	Of what? White folks? They're more afraid of me. Pain? Every whipping's got to come to an end.

PHEBE	I heard you've been whipped so many times, they lost count.
AUGUSTUS	They think they can beat me to my senses. Then they look into my eyes and see I'm not afraid.
PHEBE	It'd be something, not to be afraid.
AUGUSTUS	You have to have a purpose. Something bigger than anything they can do to you.
PHEBE	(suppressing a shudder) And ain't nobody ever tried to kill you?
AUGUSTUS	Oh, yes. First time, I was hardly alive. They ripped me from my mother the night I was born and threw me out like trash. I didn't walk until I was three.
PHEBE	Lord have mercy.
AUGUSTUS	Mercy had nothing to do with it! Missy couldn't stand the sight of me. Just look at me! It's an old story. You've stopped trembling. Now why don't you tell me

AUGUSTUS
(con't.)

what made you quake that way
in the first place?

(PHEBE shakes her head.)

Conjuration, I imagine?
Mumble-jumble from that hateful woman.

PHEBE

Her name's Scylla.

AUGUSTUS

Women like her, hah!
They get a chill one morning,
hear an owl or two, and snap!—
they've received their "powers"!
Then they collect a few old bones,
dry some herbs, and they're in business.

PHEBE

She told me to watch my footsteps—

AUGUSTUS

—or you'd fall lame.

PHEBE

And to keep my mouth shut
when the wind blowed—

AUGUSTUS

—or else the wind spirit
would steal your soul.

PHEBE

How'd you know?

AUGUSTUS

You think she's the only conjure woman
in the world? Why, your Scylla's a baby
compared to the Voodoo chiefs in the
                                    islands.

They can kill you with a puff of smoke
from their pipes—if you believe in them.
Take me: I've been cursed enough times
to bring down a whole fleet of ships
around me—but here I sit, high and dry.
So I guess they must be saving me
for something special.

*(PHEBE looks at AUGUSTUS in wonder; the
lights dim as the other SLAVES slowly come
on stage, singing as they take their places in
the fields. The song sung during the "shout"
has modulated into a percussive piece with no
words—clapping, sighs, whispered exclamations
and grunts punctuate what becomes a work song.)*

SLAVES

No way out, gotta keep on—
No way but to see it through.

NARRATOR

Don't sass, don't fight!
Lay low, grin bright!

NARRATOR
& SLAVES

No way but to see it through.

ACT I
SCENE FIVE

THE COTTON FIELDS

(The light brightens: High noon. JONES enters, looks at the sun and cracks his whip as he calls out.)

JONES

Noon!

(He exits, wiping his brow with a huge hand-kerchief. The slaves groan and sigh as they settle down with their provisions—cornpone and salt pork and gourds of water.)

ALEXANDER

(making sure that JONES is out of earshot)

I swear on all my years
there's nothing I hate so much as cotton.
Picking, toting, weighing, tramping:
the work keeps coming.

SCIPIO

No end in sight, and that's the truth!

(leans back, hands under head)

Now what I'd fancy is a life at sea.
Sun and sky and blue water,
with just a sip of rum
every once in a while.
You been to sea, Augustus.
What's it like?

AUGUSTUS	It ain't the easy life.
SCIPIO	But what's it like, man? The closest I been to the sea was when the cotton gin came in to Charleston port. All those fine flapping sails and tall masts, cotton bales stacked to heaven . . . Did you visit lots of strange places?
AUGUSTUS	We sailed the West Indies route. Stocked up rum, tobacco, beads—
SCYLLA	*(scathingly)* —and traded them for slaves. Did you have to ride cargo?
AUGUSTUS	*(with a sharp look, sarcastically)* Cap'n Newcastle was a generous master. *(resuming his story)* But those ports! Sand so white, from far off it looked like spilled cream. Palm trees taller than our masts, loaded with coconuts.
DIANA	What's a coconut?
AUGUSTUS	It's a big brown gourd with hair on it like a dog,

AUGUSTUS (con't.)	and when you break it open sweet milk pours out.
DIANA	What does it taste like?
AUGUSTUS	It tastes like . . . just coconut. There's nothing like it.
SCYLLA	Your stories stir up trouble, young man.

(*PHEBE moves as if to stop him; he motions her back.*)

AUGUSTUS	Seems you're the only one who's riled up, Scylla.
SCYLLA	You're what we call an uppity nigger. And uppity niggers always trip themselves up.
AUGUSTUS	Are you going to put a curse on me, too, Scylla? Cross your eyes and wave a few roots in the air until I fall on my knees?
SCYLLA	No need to curse you; you been cursed already.
AUGUSTUS	You feed on ignorance and call it magic. What kind of prophet works against her own people?

(The slaves murmur. SCYLLA stands up.)

SCYLLA   Oh, you may dance now,
but you will fall.
The evil inside you
will cut you down to your knees,
and you will crawl—crawl in front of
us all!

(Lights dim, then grow mottled and swamp green as all exit.)

ACT I
SCENE SIX

THE SWAMP

(Light mottled and swamp green. Night sounds filter in as HECTOR enters.)

HECTOR

Easy, easy: Don't tell the cook
the meat's gone bad.

(slashes at the underbrush)

We got to cut it out.
Ya! Ya!

(hacks in rhythm for a moment)

I can still smell it. Pah!

(sniffs, then peers)

But there's a rose in the gravy, oh yes—
a rose shining through the mists, a red smell.
Red and mean.

But how sweet she smelled!
Cottons and flowers.
And lemons that bite back
when you touch them to the tongue.

Shh! Don't tell the cook.
Black folks fiddle, the white folks stare.

(*There is a bird call; HECTOR conceals him-self. AUGUSTUS enters; he appears to be fol-lowing the sound. He gives out a matching call, then bursts into a clearing in the swamp where a group of black men sit in a circle around a small fire, chanting softly.*)

LEADER   (*rises*)

There you are!
We've called two nights.

AUGUSTUS   Who are you?

LEADER   Patience, Augustus Newcastle.
Oh yes, we know all about you.

AUGUSTUS   What do you want?

LEADER   Your courage has been a beacon—

CONSPIRATORS   Amen! Selah!

(*The CONSPIRATORS surround the LEADER; they react to his words in a call-and-response fashion; their movements are vaguely ritualis-tic and creepy, as if they were under a spell; this can be enhanced with dance and pantomime. AUGUSTUS stands still as the CONSPIRA-TORS swarm around him, occasionally trying to pull him among them.*)

LEADER	—and we need men willing to fight for freedom! Tell me, Augustus Newcastle: are you prepared to sign your name with the revolutionary forces?
AUGUSTUS	First tell me who you are.
LEADER	So cautious? We expected a bit more daring from someone of your reputation.
AUGUSTUS	I am many things, but I'm not a fool.
LEADER	*(laughs)*
	Shall we show him, brothers?
CONSPIRATORS	Selah!
LEADER	Each of us has been called forth as a warrior of righteousness. Each wandered in darkness until he found the light of brotherhood! Take young Benjamin Skeene:
	(BENJAMIN squares his shoulders as he steps forward; he is a trim young man who, judging from his clothes, must be either a house slave or a freeman.)
	As a skilled carpenter, he enjoys a fair amount of freedom.

BENJAMIN	The boss man's glad I can make his deliveries.
LEADER	So we've arranged a few deposits of our own. Benjamin, can you find a way to fasten this blade to a pole?
BENJAMIN	Easy.
LEADER	Every man who can wield a stick shall have a bayonet!
CONSPIRATORS	Selah!
LEADER	A few were more reluctant . . . or shall I say cautious? Henry Blake, for instance: (HENRY, *a dark middle-aged man, steps forward hesitantly.*) Fear had made him grateful for every crumb his master dropped him. (*The two act out the following exchange.*)
HENRY	I don't want no part of this!
LEADER	You followed the sign; you have been called!

HENRY	Any fool knows a mockingbird when he hears one—and that weren't no mockingbird!
LEADER	(threatening)
	Are you prepared to slay our oppressors, male and female, when it is deemed time, according to the plans of insurrection drawn up and approved by members present?
HENRY	I'm against the white man much as all of you—but murder? "Thou shalt not kill," saith the Commandments.
LEADER	Who made your master?
HENRY	God.
LEADER	And who made you?
HENRY	God.
LEADER	Then aren't you as good as your master if God made you both?
HENRY	I'm not a vengeful man.
LEADER	But our Lord is a vengeful God. "Whoever steals a man," He says,

"whether he sells him or
is found in possession of him,
shall be put to death."

Who is not with us
is against us.
You answered the call.
If you turn back now . . .

(HENRY *slowly lifts his head, squares his shoulders,
and remains frozen in the spotlight while the
LEADER speaks to AUGUSTUS.*)

LEADER	He was brought to reason.
CONSPIRATORS	Selah.
LEADER	So the one becomes many and the many, one. Hence our password: "May Fate be with you—
CONSPIRATORS	And with us all!"
AUGUSTUS	Now I see who you are.
LEADER	Augustus Newcastle: Are you prepared to slay our oppressors, male and female, when it is deemed time, according to the plans of insurrection drawn up and approved by members present?

AUGUSTUS	I am.
LEADER	Enter your name in the Book of Redemption!
	(AUGUSTUS signs the book.)
CONSPIRATORS	Selah! Selah!
AUGUSTUS	Tell me what to do.
LEADER	You'll need a second-in-command. Report your choice to us; we will send out the sign. *(turning to the group)* My brothers, it is time to be free! Maps are being prepared of the city and its surroundings along with the chief points of attack. Bullets wait in kegs under the dock. Destiny calls!
CONSPIRATORS	Amen!
LEADER	There are barrels of gun powder stacked in a cave outside Dawson's Plantation. Our Toby has been busy— *(CONSPIRATORS nod and laugh in consent.)*

but he cannot risk further expeditions.
Henry Blake!

(HENRY steps forward.)

Your owner praised you in the marketplace
as the most trustworthy nigger
he ever had the fortune of owning.
Now it is up to you
to put your master's trust to the test.

*(HENRY bows his head in assent, steps back
into the group.)*

LEADER   Destiny calls us! The reckoning is nigh!
But remember: trust no one.
All those who are not with us
are against us, blacks as well
as whites. Oh, do not falter!
Bolster your heart with the memory
of the atrocities committed upon your mothers.
Gird your loins with vengeance,
strap on the shining sword of freedom!

CONSPIRATORS   Selah!

LEADER   Brothers, are you with me?

CONSPIRATORS   Right behind you!

LEADER   Then nothing can stop us now!

AUGUSTUS	*(blurts out)*
	My orders! What are my orders?
LEADER	*(a little taken aback, but decides on the role of the amused patriarch)*
	Patience, my son! Patience and cunning. Sow discontent among your brethren, inspire them to fury.
AUGUSTUS	I can do more. Read maps, write passes—
LEADER	That is all for now. Is that clear?
	(Strained silence; the LEADER speaks reassuringly.)
	You will recognize the signal.
	(The CONSPIRATORS begin humming "Steal Away".)
LEADER	Go to your people and test their minds; so when the fires of redemption lick the skies of Charleston, they will rise up, up— a mighty army marching into battle!

CONSPIRATORS	Steal away, steal away, Steal away to Jesus! Steal away, steal away home, I ain't got long to stay here.

(*The CONSPIRATORS continue singing as they exchange farewells and slip off. HECTOR appears at the edge of the undergrowth, a dead snake in his outstretched arms.*)

(*BLACKOUT.*)

ACT I
SCENE SEVEN

THE COTTON FIELDS

NARRATOR

A sniff of freedom's all it takes
to feel history's sting;
there's danger by-and-by
when the slaves won't sing.

(JONES supervises the picking, which transpires without singing; the silence is eerie. JONES's appearance is slovenly, as if he's already been drinking.)

JONES

Move it, nigger! Faster!
What you glaring at? Faster!

(The SLAVES continue picking at the same rate. JONES looks at the sun, then cracks his whip)

Aw, the hell with ya! Noon!

(He stumbles offstage. The SLAVES divide into two groups: Some hum spirituals while the others gather around AUGUSTUS.)

SCIPIO

Come on, Augustus, what else?

AUGUSTUS

Did you know there are slaves
who have set themselves free?

SCIPIO

(almost afraid to ask)

How'd they do that?

AUGUSTUS

Santo Domingo, San Domingue, Hispaniola—
three names for an island
rising like a fortress
from the waters of the Caribbean.
An island of sun and forest,
wild fruit and mosquitoes—
and slaves, many slaves—half a million.
Slaves to chop sugar, slaves
to pick coffee beans, slaves to do
their French masters' every bidding.

Then one summer, news came
from the old country: Revolution!
Plantation owners broke into a sweat;
their slaves served cool drinks
while the masters rocked on their verandas,
discussing each outrage:
people marching against the king,
crowds pouring into the streets,
shouting three words:
Liberté!

SLAVES

We shall be free!

AUGUSTUS

Égalité!

SLAVES

Master and slave.

AUGUSTUS

Fraternité!

SLAVES	Brothers and sisters!
AUGUSTUS	Liberté, Égalité, Fraternité—three words were all the island masters talked about that summer, while their slaves served carefully and listened.
SLAVES	Liberté, Égalité, Fraternité!

(During the following speech, a smoldering growl among the slaves grows louder and louder, until it explodes in a shout.)

AUGUSTUS	Black men meeting in the forest: Eight days, they whispered, and we'll be free. For eight days bonfires flashed in the hills: Equality. For eight days tom-toms spoke in the mountains: Liberty. For eight days the tom-toms sang: Brothers and sisters. And on the eighth day, swift as lightning, the slaves attacked.
SLAVES	Yah!

(AMALIA enters, unseen, and stands listening.)

AUGUSTUS	They came down the mountains to the sound of tambourines and conch shells. With torches they swept onto the plantations, with the long harvest knives

they chopped white men down
like sugar cane. For three weeks
the flames raged; then the sun
broke through the smoke and shone
upon a new nation, a black nation—
Haiti!

SLAVES   Haiti!

AUGUSTUS   (looking intently at the faces around him)

                Now do you see
                why they've kept this from us,
                brothers and sisters?

AMALIA   A lovely speech.

                (The slaves are horrified. AUGUSTUS stands
                impassive.)

                I see you're a poet
                as well as a rebel.

                (JONES rushes in.)

JONES   Anything wrong, Miss Jennings?

AMALIA   Not a thing, Jones. Just passing
                the time of day with my happy flock—
                which is more than I see you doing.

JONES   But it's noon, Miss Jennings!
                They need nourishment
                if we're going to get this crop in.

AMALIA	It appears they've been getting a different sort of sustenance.
JONES	*(uncomprehending)*
	Beg pardon, Ma'am?
AMALIA	*(impatient with JONES)*

See that they work an extra hour tonight.
I don't care if they have to pick
                              by moonlight!

(to AUGUSTUS)

As for you: I'll see you
up at the house. Come at sunset—
the view over the fields
is most enchanting then.

(She strides off. BLACKOUT.)

ACT I
SCENE EIGHT

THE BIG HOUSE:
Louis's study; parlor

(Twilight filters through the curtains; the frogs have started up in the swamp.)

(LOUIS paces back and forth in his room, holding a chart; he stops to stare at it for a moment, then waves it in disgust and paces once more.)

LOUIS

Something's out there: I can feel it!
What a discovery it would be.
But no—

(grabs his brandy)

no new coin shines
for Louis LaFarge
among the stars!

(He stops at the window and stares out.)

(AMALIA sits in the parlor reading, a decanter of sherry and a tea service on the table next to the sofa. The evening song of the slaves floats in from the fields—a plaintive air with a compelling affirmation of life, a strange melody with no distinct beat or tune. TICEY, the old house slave, enters.)

TICEY	Miss Amalia?
AMALIA	*(without turning)*
	Yes?
TICEY	That new slave, Ma'am—
	he's standing at the front porch!
AMALIA	*(amused)*
	The front porch? Well, show him in, Ticey!
	(TICEY exits; AMALIA rises and goes to the window. She is looking out toward the fields when AUGUSTUS appears in the doorway. Although she knows he is there, she does not turn around.)
AMALIA	What are they singing?
AUGUSTUS	No words you'd understand.
	No tune you'd recognize.
AMALIA	And how is it they all sing together?
AUGUSTUS	It's the sorrow songs.
	They don't need a psalm book.
AMALIA	*(resumes her imperious manner)*
	"Personal servant to Captain Newcastle of the schooner Victoria. Ports of call: St. Thomas, Tobago, St. Croix, Martinique"—in other words, a slave ship.

AUGUSTUS	Yes.
AMALIA	And what did you learn under your captain's tutelage?
AUGUSTUS	Reading. Writing. Figures.
AMALIA	What did you read?
AUGUSTUS	Milton. The Bible. And the Tales of the Greeks.
AMALIA	*(thrusting the book she's been reading at him)* See the blue ribbon sticking out? You may start there. *(AUGUSTUS turns the book over to read the title, then looks at her for a moment before returning it. She snatches the book.)*
AMALIA	Too difficult? No doubt you'd do better with the Greek original— *(slyly)* but we are not that cultured a household. *(circling him)* I wondered could there be a nigger alive smart as this one's claimed to be? Of course, if there were, he might be smart enough to pretend he wasn't smart at all.

AUGUSTUS	No pretense. I've read that one already. In my opinion, the Greeks were a bit too predictable.
AMALIA	A slave has no opinion!
	(*regaining her composure*)
	I could have you flogged to your bones for what you did today.
AUGUSTUS	Why didn't you?
	(*The SLAVES stop singing.*)
AMALIA	Daddy said a master knows his slaves better than they know themselves. And he never flogged a slave— he said it was a poor businessman who damaged his own merchandise.
AUGUSTUS	(*sarcastically*)
	An enlightened man, your father.
AMALIA	He let me run wild until it was time to put on crinolines. My playmates were sent to the fields, and I was sent to the parlor with needlework— a scented, dutiful daughter.

AUGUSTUS	Most men find intelligence troubling in a woman—even fathers.
AMALIA	Then, off I went to finishing school: Miss Peeters' Academy for Elocution and Deportment! "The art of conversation," she used to say —please, sit down!—"is to make the passing of time agreeable."

(arranging her dress as she sits on the sofa)

"Suitable subjects are—"
Sit down, I said!

(softer, but with an edge)

 One does not conduct conversation
while standing.

(She indicates a chair, upholstered in champagne colored tufted damask. AUGUSTUS moves toward it but swiftly and gracefully drops cross-legged to the floor, daringly close to AMALIA's slippered feet. She starts to pull away—then slowly extends her feet again.)

"Suitable subjects for
genteel conversation are:

(ticking them off on her fingers)

"Nature. Travel. History.
And above all, culture—
painting, music, and books."

AMALIA (con't.)	Well, we're done with books! Tell me, Mr. Newcastle— was the weather in the Indies very different from here?
AUGUSTUS	Warmer.
AMALIA	Is that all?
AUGUSTUS	There was always a breeze.
AMALIA	And an abundance of exotic foods, I'm sure.
AUGUSTUS	We had our share of papaya. *(The SLAVES start up a new song, more African in rhythm and harmonies.)*
AMALIA	Imagine that. Subject number two: Travel. So many ports! *(shaking her head charmingly)* Did Captain Newcastle allow you to go ashore at St. Thomas, Tobago, Martinique?
AUGUSTUS	*(on guard)* No.
AMALIA	Charleston has welcomed a fair share of immigrants to her shores.

(laughs delicately)

There was that Haiti business around the time
I was born. Over five hundred French
                                    plantation owners
fled here. The whole city was in panic.
Why, my dear husband—hear him pacing
up there, wearing out the floorboards?—
little Louis showed up in Charleston harbor
that year, with his blue blood *maman* and *papa*.
Liberté, Égalité, Fraternité!

(looking directly at AUGUSTUS)

It was a brilliant revolution.
I've often wondered why our niggers
don't revolt. I've said to myself:
"Amalia, if you had been a slave,
you most certainly would have plotted
an insurrection by now."

(turns away from AUGUSTUS)

But we say all sorts of things
to ourselves, don't we?
There's no telling what we'd do
if the moment were there for the taking.

*(lights up on LOUIS, still staring out the
window)*

LOUIS

You can't hide forever.
There's a hole in the heavens,
and you're throbbing right behind it.

LOUIS (con't.)	*(whispers)*
	I can feel you.
AMALIA	Have you ever heard of the Amistad?
AUGUSTUS	Why?
AMALIA	The Amistad: a slave ship. Three days off the port of Principe the Africans freed themselves and attacked with machetes and harpoons. Cinque, their leader, spared two sailors to steer them back to Africa. But Cinque was unfamiliar with the stars in our hemisphere. Each morning he set course east by the sun; each night the sailors turned the ship and steered west—until they managed to land on our coast and deliver Cinque and his followers to execution.
AUGUSTUS	A bit of a storybook ending, isn't it?
AMALIA	What's that supposed to mean?
AUGUSTUS	It's just so perfect a lesson.
AMALIA	You don't believe me? It was in the newspapers. *(significantly)* You followed your precious captain everywhere; you were there when

88

he loaded slave cargo into the hold
or plotted a new course.
What an admirable science, navigation!
It must be terribly complicated,
even for you.

AUGUSTUS   *(getting up from the floor)*

Now I have a story for you.
Once there was a preacher slave
went by the name of Isaac.
When God called him
he was a boy, out hunting rice birds.
Killing rice birds is easy—
just pinch off their heads.

(indicating the sherry)

May I?

*(AMALIA flinches, nods. He pours the sherry
expertly.)*

But one day, halfway up the tree
where a nest of babies chirped,
a voice called out: "Don't do it, Isaac."
It was an angel, shining
in the crook of a branch.
Massa let him preach.
What harm could it do?

(sitting down in the damask chair)

AUGUSTUS
(con't.)

Then a slave uprising in Virginia
had all the white folks
watching their own niggers
for signs of treachery.
No more prayer meetings, Isaac!
But God would not wait,
so Isaac kept on preaching
at night, in the woods.

Of course he was caught.
Three of his congregation
were shot on the spot, three others branded
and their feet pierced.
But what to do about Isaac,
gentle Isaac who had turned traitor?

AMALIA

Is there a point to this?

AUGUSTUS

I'm just passing the time of evening
with . . . conversation.

(Upstairs, LOUIS positions his telescope at the window and searches the heavens.)

LOUIS

There it is . . . no, wait!
Gone.

(shakes his head in despair)

Sometimes I catch
a glimmer, a hot blue flash—
then it disappears.
Show yourself, demon!

(In the parlor, AUGUSTUS takes a sip of sherry and continues.)

AUGUSTUS

First they flogged him. Then
they pickled the wounds with salt water,
and when they were nearly healed,
he was flogged again, and the wounds
pickled again, and on and on for weeks
while Massa sold off Isaac's children
one at a time. They took him to see
his wife on the auction block,
baby at her breast.
A week later it was his turn.
His back had finally healed;
but as his new owner led him
from the auction block,
Isaac dropped down dead.

(pause; more to himself than to AMALIA)

They couldn't break his spirit,
so they broke his heart.

(They stare at each other for a moment; then AMALIA rises and walks to the window. It has gotten dark outside.)

AMALIA

They're still singing.
How can they have songs left?

AUGUSTUS

(joining her at the window)

As many songs as sorrows.

AMALIA	And you, Augustus? Were you ever happy?
AUGUSTUS	Happy? No.
AMALIA	Never? Not even on the ship with the whole sea around you?
AUGUSTUS	I was a boy. I felt lucky, not happy.
AMALIA	I was happy once. I traded it for luck.
AUGUSTUS	Luck's a dangerous master.
AMALIA	Half my life I spent dreaming, the other half burying dreams. *(bitter laugh, turns to AUGUSTUS)* Funny, isn't it?
AUGUSTUS	*(turns away from her with difficulty, stares out the window)* One soft spring night when the pear blossoms cast their pale faces on the darker face of the earth, Massa stood up from the porch swing and said to himself, "I think I'll make me another bright-eyed pickaninny." Then he stretched and headed for my mother's cabin. And now— that pickaninny, who started out no more than the twinkle in a white man's eye

and the shame between his mama's legs—
now he stands in the parlor of
another massa, entertaining the pretty mistress
with stories of whippings and heartbreak.

AMALIA

(half to herself)

Pretty? Am I pretty?

AUGUSTUS

(answers in spite of himself)

You can put a rose in a vase
with a bunch of other flowers;
but when you walk into the room
the rose is the only thing you see.

(AMALIA touches his wrist, then traces the vein up his arm, as if remembering.)

AMALIA

Imagine! A life without even
a smidgen of happiness . . .

AUGUSTUS

(wrestling with desire)

I'm not one of your dreams.

AMALIA

No? Perhaps not. What a pity.

(She touches his cheek; he holds her hand there. They lean towards each other slowly, as the slaves' sorrow song surges—but before their lips touch, there is BLACKOUT.)

E N D   O F   A C T   I

A C T   I I
S C E N E   O N E

D R E A M   S E Q U E N C E

(Dimly lit, the light rather blue. Each group is in its appointed "place" on stage—AMALIA in her parlor with TICEY standing impassively in the background; LOUIS above, in his study; most slaves going about their chores; SCYLLA isolated, with her herbs and potions. In the swamp, HECTOR searches for snakes; the CONSPIRATORS huddle, occasionally lifting a fist into the circle. AUGUSTUS stands front and center, back to the audience, gazing at AMALIA. Mostly silhouettes are seen, except when a single voice rises out of the chanting, which will grow to cacophony at the end of the sequence.)

SLAVES	They have bowed our heads,
	They have bent our backs.
	Mercy, mercy,
	Lord above, mercy.
AMALIA	I slept, but my heart was awake.
	How beautiful he is!
SLAVES	Lord have mercy.
	They have bowed our heads . . .
SCYLLA	There's a curse on the land.
	The net draws closer.
HECTOR	Under rocks, 'twixt reeds and roots . . .
SLAVES	They have bent our backs,
	They have snatched our songs . . .
	(humming, "Sometimes I feel like a motherless child"; gradually adding words)

Sometimes I feel like a motherless child,
A motherless child, a motherless child,
Sometimes I feel like a motherless child—

LOUIS

(in a scientific voice, detached, as if reciting)

Every night at the same hour, each star appears slightly to the west of its previous position. Scientists calculate that the twelve houses of the zodiac have shifted so radically since ancient times, their relation to each other may now signify completely different portents.

HECTOR

So many, so many.

SLAVES

"A long way from home."

AUGUSTUS

One soft night, Massa stood up—

CONSPIRATORS

Selah.

AUGUSTUS

—and laughed to himself.

CONSPIRATORS

It is time.

SCYLLA

The net draws tighter.

CONSPIRATORS

Selah!

AUGUSTUS

One darkening evening, I stood up—

(SLAVES humming, CONSPIRATORS chanting "Selah" in a barely audible whisper)

AUGUSTUS

—and she was mine,
mine all night, until
the day breathed fire
and the shadows fled.

AMALIA	Look, how beautiful he is!
CONSPIRATORS	Rise up!
SLAVES	*(simultaneously)*
	Mercy, mercy.
AMALIA	His eyes, his brow, his cheeks—
CONSPIRATORS	Rise up!
AMALIA	his lips . . .
AUGUSTUS	. . . until the day breathed fire . . .
HECTOR	Eshu Elewa . . . ogo . . . gbogbo.
SLAVES	They have bowed our heads, They have bent our backs.
SCYLLA	Closer . . .
	(PHEBE dashes to center stage, hands outstretched as if to hold back a flood.)
PHEBE	Stop it! Stop!!!
	(Everyone freezes.)

ACT II

SCENE TWO

AT THE SLAVE CABINS

(PHEBE drops her arms and moves slightly stage left. AUGUSTUS, with his back still to the audience, backs downstage, looking alternately at AMALIA and the CONSPIRATORS until the tableau disintegrates. PHEBE taps him on the shoulder, and he whirls around.)

PHEBE	Evenin'.
AUGUSTUS	Oh! Phebe. Evening.
PHEBE	You're trembling.
AUGUSTUS	I am?
	(laughs)
	Cold spell coming on, I imagine.
PHEBE	No, that's what you said to me!
	(AUGUSTUS looks at her, uncomprehending.)
	That time I was coming back from Scylla's, scared to open my mouth, you said: "What's your hurry?" And then you said, "You're trembling," and I said, "I am?" —just like you did now.

AUGUSTUS	Oh.
PHEBE	What's your hurry? Heading up to the House again?
AUGUSTUS	I got a moment.
PHEBE	Sit yourself down, then. Rest a spell. *(They sit side by side; PHEBE embarrassed,* *AUGUSTUS nervous.)*
PHEBE	You sure be up there a long time. At the Big House, I mean.
AUGUSTUS	*(tersely)* Missy's orders.
PHEBE	What else she have you doing?
AUGUSTUS	We practice the fine art of conversation.
PHEBE	Quit fooling!
AUGUSTUS	Oh, yes, we talk about everything— weather and the science of navigation, recent history and ancient literature.
PHEBE	What's that she-fox up to now?
AUGUSTUS	It's simple: she wants to tame me. And if I get better treatment than the rest of you,

	all my talk about Haiti won't hold much water.
PHEBE	So she think she can get us to fighting amongst ourselves!
AUGUSTUS	Seems plenty folks want things just the way they are. Alexander keeps his distance, lately.
PHEBE	Alexander's seen his share of sorrow. He just wants to live in peace.
AUGUSTUS	And die in peace?
PHEBE	*(not catching his drift)*
	I 'spect so. Who doesn't? Oh, that's right— you and Death gonna walk outta here hand and hand!
	(laughs; AUGUSTUS is spooked)
	Alexander don't mean you no spite. And Scipio—Scipio say you his man, any time, any place! You shoulda seen him the other day, putting voodoo spells on the chickens! Then he pick up the milk bucket and pranced around, serving up revolution lemonade! Now there's a body need of some occupation!

AUGUSTUS	(aside) Maybe I can help him find it.
PHEBE	Course, you got Diana's heart. She think the sun and the moon set in your face.
AUGUSTUS	Then there's Scylla.
PHEBE	Hmmpf! Woman had me nearly crazy, clamping my mouth and wiping my footsteps so I ended up getting nowhere. As far as I'm concerned, Scylla can roll her eye and talk conjuration till the summer go cold and the cotton pick itself!
AUGUSTUS	Now, that's the fire I saw!
PHEBE	Huh?
AUGUSTUS	The first time I saw you, I thought to myself: "That's not the spirit of a slave. That's a pure flame." (PHEBE tucks her head, flattered.) Tell me—how did you land on the Jennings plantation?
PHEBE	I didn't land at all. I was borned here.

AUGUSTUS	So this is your home.
PHEBE	Much as any of us got a home on this earth.
AUGUSTUS	And your folks?
PHEBE	My father was sold before I was borned. Mama . . . it's a long story.
AUGUSTUS	I got time.

(PHEBE stares down at the ground as if she's conjuring the memory out of the dust; then she begins.)

PHEBE	Mama worked in the kitchen until I was about five; that's when fever broke out in the quarters. She used to set table scraps out for the field hands, and I stuck wildflowers in the baskets to pretty 'em up. Mama said you never know what a flower can mean to somebody in misery.

That fever tore through the cabins like wildfire.
Massa Jennings said the field hands
spread contamination and forbid them
to come up to the house, but
Mama couldn't stand watching them
just wasting away—so she started
sneaking food to the quarters at night.

PHEBE (con't.)   Then the fever caught her, too.
                   She couldn't hide it long.
                   And Massa Jennings found out.

                   (gulps a deep breath for strength, reliving the scene)

                   Mama started wailing right there at the stove.
                   Hadn't she been a good servant?
                   Who stayed up three nights straight
                   to keep Massa's baby girl among the living
                   when her own mother done left this world?
                   Who did he call when the fire
                   needed lighting? Who mended the pinafores
                   Miss Amalia was forever snagging on bushes?

                   Mama dropped to her knees
                   and stretched out her arms along the floor.
                   She didn't have nowheres to go;
                   she'd always been at the Big House.
                   "Where am I gonna lay
                   my poor sick head?" she asked.

                   He stood there, staring
                   like she was a rut in the road,
                   and he was trying to figure out
                   how to get around it.

                   Then he straightened his waistcoat
                   and said: "You have put me and my child
                   in the path of mortal danger,
                   and you dare ask me what to do
                   with your nappy black head?"

He didn't even look at her—
just spoke off into the air
like she was already a ghost.

(woodenly)

She died soon after.

AUGUSTUS   *(takes PHEBE into his arms, a bit helplessly)*

Lord have mercy.

PHEBE   Mercy had nothing to do with it.
Ain't that what you said?

AUGUSTUS   Phebe, how far would you go
to avenge your mother's death?

PHEBE   There you go again
with your revolution talk.

AUGUSTUS   How far?

PHEBE   We ain't got no tom-toms
like them slaves in Haiti!

AUGUSTUS   You don't need tom-toms.
Just a bird call.

(PHEBE looks at him, uncomprehending. AUGUSTUS stares off.)

(Stage dims to black: a single spot on the NARRATOR.)

NARRATOR | What is it about him, girl—
the book-learning, his acquaintance with
the world?

He can stand up to a glare,
but he doesn't know his heart.
Look around you, child: it's growing dark.

A C T   I I
S C E N E   T H R E E

T H E   C O T T O N   H O U S E

(Almost sundown: JONES is in the field supervising the bringing in of the cotton, which has been weighed and now must be tramped down in order to be stored. There is the steady beat of stomping feet throughout the scene. PHEBE and AUGUSTUS outside the cotton house.)

PHEBE

Any news?

AUGUSTUS

Henry's bringing another wagonload in.

PHEBE

(glancing at the sky with jealousy and trepidation)

You better get on up there—
sun's almost touching.

(PHEBE scoots inside the cotton house. AUGUSTUS studies the horizon, his expression inexplicable, then exits as JONES enters from the fields, urging along the next group bearing cotton. The SLAVES are sweaty and tired. JONES looks after AUGUSTUS; it's clear he's been told not to interfere.)

JONES

Keep it moving!
Don't be looking at the sun;
you got a whole long while
before your day is over!

(*JONES exits.. The scene opens to the inside of the cotton house; SCIPIO dumps the sacks of cotton onto the floor while the other slaves tramp it down. The dull thud of stomping feet punctuates the dialogue; changes in pace and rhythm signal changes in mood and tension. On his way for the next sack of cotton, SCIPIO looks out the one small window.*)

SCIPIO

There he goes.

ALEXANDER

Every evening, same time.

SCYLLA

It's the devil's work afoot, for sure.

SCIPIO

It *is* peculiar!
I wonder—

PHEBE

It ain't your task to wonder.

SCIPIO

What's the matter with you, gal?
Most times you're the one speculating
about other folks' doings.
Maybe you're sweet on him.

(*General laughter.*)

PHEBE

If you ain't finding fault with someone,
you all laughing at them! We all been
called up to the house one time or another.
Ain't nothing special in that.

SCYLLA	For weeks on end? As soon as the sun eases into the sycamores, there ain't a hair of his to be seen till daylight.
	(significant pause)
	Except maybe on his lady's pillow.
PHEBE	What you trying to say, Scylla?
SCYLLA	I ain't *trying* to say nothing.
ALEXANDER	He's certainly the boldest nigger I've ever seen.
SCIPIO	*(shaking his head in admiration)*
	That's the truth there! The way he handles Massa Jones— no bowing or scraping for him. That eye of his could cut through stone. Jones don't know what to do with that nigger! He's plain scared, and that's a fact.
PHEBE	Maybe they're just talking.
DIANA	Augustus is nice.
ALEXANDER	Nice as the devil was to Eve.

SCYLLA	A slave and his missus ain't got nothing to talk about. Oh, he might have bold ideas, but he'll never put them to work. She'll see to that.
PHEBE	What do you mean?
SCYLLA	That first master of his kept him in style. That's why he ran away so much afterwards— he ain't used to being treated like a regular slave A whip can't make him behave: Miss Amalia knows that. So she's trying another way— and it appears to be working.
SCIPIO	Well, I'll be.
DIANA	What 'pears to be working?
SCYLLA	What's the only thing white folks think a nigger buck's good for? It wouldn't be the first time.
ALEXANDER	(slowly) If that's what he's doing, he's headed for big trouble.
PHEBE	I don't believe it! And even if it's true, it's 'cause he ain't got no choice!

SCYLLA	You been mighty contrary lately, Phebe.
PHEBE	I ain't afraid of every shadow!
SCIPIO	*(trying to avert disaster)*
	Scylla, don't mind her. She's feeling the weather.
SCYLLA	I'm warning you, Phebe.
PHEBE	I already got a pack of curses on my head. A few more won't hurt.
ALEXANDER	Phebe! Don't talk to Scylla like that!
PHEBE	Should have done it a long time ago. Woman had me nearly crazy! If anyone around here's putting sharp stones in my path, it ain't no earth spirit. If there's a curse here, Scylla, it's you.
	(Everyone stops stamping.)
DIANA	Phebe . . .
PHEBE	Yes, Scylla, you're the curse— with all your roots and potions. Tell me: How come you never put a spell on Miss Amalia? Why didn't you

109

PHEBE (con't.)   sprinkle some powder over a candle
to make her house go up in flames
one night? That would have been some magic.

(timid murmurs from the others)

SCYLLA   I do what the spirits tell me.

PHEBE   Then those slaves in Haiti
must have known some better spirits.

SCYLLA   Some bold nigger comes in here with
a few pretty stories,
and you think he's the Savior!

ALEXANDER   Dear Lord!

PHEBE   The Savior was never
to your liking, Scylla.
He took too much attention
away from you.

ALEXANDER   Have mercy!

SCYLLA   *(drawing herself into her full "conjurer" posture)*

There's a vine in the woods
with a leaf like a saw blade.
One side of the leaf is shiny dark
and pocked like skin;
the other side is dusty gray.
Touch the gray side to a wound,

the sore will shut and heal.
But touch it with the shiny side,
and the wound will boil up
and burst open.

PHEBE

Always talking in riddles!
Why don't you come right out and
say what you mean for a change?

(*Agreeing murmurs; SCYLLA looks darkly around
until everybody grows silent.*)

SCYLLA

All right, I'll tell you direct.
Your Augustus is pretty clever—
been lots of places and knows
the meanings of words and things like that.
But something's foul in his blood,
and what's festering inside him
nothing this side of the living
can heal. A body hurting that bad
will do anything to get relief—anything.

(*looking around at all of them*)

So keep talking about Haiti
and sharpening your sticks!
But know one thing:
that nigger's headed for destruction,
and you're all headed there with him.

(*They stare at her as the lights dim to
BLACKOUT.*)

A C T   I I
S C E N E   F O U R

T H E   S W A M P

(Night; mottled light. Strangely twisted branches, replete with Spanish moss and vines; huge gnarled roots slick with wet. The whole resembles abstract gargoyles in a gothic cathedral. There's a gigantic tree trunk which HECTOR will festoon with moss later in the scene to serve as a makeshift throne. At some remove—in front of the proscenium, or silhouetted against the backdrop—the SLAVES pantomime the motions of evening chores: mending tools, shelling beans, stirring the stew.)

(When the lights come up, Hector is puttering around the perimeter of the swamp, muttering to himself; he finds a snake and lifts it up triumphantly before whacking off the head.)

HECTOR	Hah! So many—under rocks, 'twixt reeds, they lie and breed, breed, breed. The wicked never rest.
	(stops, listens)
	What's that? Someone coming!
	(He scrambles for cover as BENJAMIN SKEENE and AUGUSTUS enter, stop, and shake hands.)
BENJAMIN	Good night, friend. We will be victorious.
AUGUSTUS	May Fate be with us, brother.

BENJAMIN	Oh she is, brother, she is. It was a golden day when Fate brought you to us. *(They exchange the secret handshake; BENJAMIN exits. AUGUSTUS looks after him; then, as soon as he thinks he's alone, he sinks down on a fallen log, burying his face in his hands. HECTOR— well hidden from AUGUSTUS but visible to the audience—looks on with keen interest; he recognizes this kind of despair. AUGUSTUS's soliloquy is more an agitated outpouring than a reflective speech.)*
AUGUSTUS	Compass and sextant. Ropes thick as my wrist, coiled like greased snakes. A cutlass. The rough caress of the anchor line slithering between my boy palms. The hourglass tipped, surrendering sand in a thin stream of sighs. Clouded belly of the gas lamp dangling from a chain. And everything rocking, rocking. *(hums a lullaby)* Dark green pillows, salve for my wounds. "Who did this to you, boy?" "It was the sun, Father; see its spokes?" "Child of midnight, the sun can't hurt you!" *(sings softly)* "Jesus Savior pilot me over Life's tempestuous sea . . ."

AUGUSTUS (con't.)	(*speaks*) And when she looks at me— such a cool sweet look— each scar weeps like an open wound. (*softer*) If fear eats out the heart, what does love do? (*HECTOR springs out of hiding; AUGUSTUS jumps up.*)
HECTOR	You! I've seen you before.
AUGUSTUS	(*relieved*) That you have, my friend. I'm from the Jennings Plantation, like you.
HECTOR	(*stares at him suspiciously*) Like me? Like me you say? We'll see about that. (*circles him, inspecting*) What are you doing in my swamp?
AUGUSTUS	Taking a walk. Breathing the night air.
HECTOR	Wrong! You were with someone. I saw you!

AUGUSTUS	Just a friend, Hector. Don't you have friends?
HECTOR	I saw you. I heard you! How do you know my name?
AUGUSTUS	We met before; don't you remember? I'm the new slave on the Jennings Plantation.
HECTOR	You're the one who came in leg irons, along the road—

(circling him very closely, so that AUGUSTUS must back up)

I never heard of leg irons on this plantation
$$\text{before.}$$

(crowds AUGUSTUS, who trips on a root and falls)

You must be dangerous.

AUGUSTUS	I was sold in chains and spent my first night in the barn. The overseer didn't have enough sense to take them off until Amalia gave the order—
HECTOR	Amalia? Amalia! You are plotting some evil.
AUGUSTUS	You've got swamp fever, old man. I plan no evil.

HECTOR	I heard you! Men come and go in wagons. They whisper and shake hands. They come out at night when the innocent sleep.
AUGUSTUS	These men—what do they look like?
HECTOR	They have the devil's eye.
AUGUSTUS	Are they black men, or white?
HECTOR	You are one of them!
AUGUSTUS	If they are black, black like me and you, how can they be evil?
HECTOR	*(vehemently)* No, no—the world's not right, don't you see? I took the curse as far away as I could.
AUGUSTUS	There is no curse!
HECTOR	*(draping moss and vines over the tree trunk to make a "throne")* Ah, but the little mother's gone. And I came here, where evil bubbles out of the ground. Once I didn't watch out; I got lost in the smell of a rose

and snap!—the snake bit down.
Little mother was mother no more.

AUGUSTUS

I'm no snake, Hector.

HECTOR

Evil isn't the snake, little man.
Evil is what grows the snake.

(gazing into the distance)

Such a cool sweet look . . .

(cuts a piercing glance at AUGUSTUS, who recognizes his own words and is on guard— though against what, he's not sure)

AUGUSTUS

You *are* crazy.

HECTOR

Once we had a garden to hide in,
but we were children.

(taking his seat on the throne; with a full sweep of his arm)

This is my home now.
I am king here.

(regarding him suspiciously)

Every man has his place.

AUGUSTUS

And you are fortunate to have found yours.
They've left you in peace.
But what of your brothers and sisters?
They cry out in their bondage.

AUGUSTUS (con't.)	They have no place in this world to lay their heads.
HECTOR	*(in a low growl)* You are planning a great evil. You come out at night when the innocent sleep— *(raising his voice)* but I won't let you harm her!
AUGUSTUS	Sshh! Someone might hear.
HECTOR	I won't let you harm her! *(screaming)* Danger! Wake up, children! *(The SLAVES wake up and stumble to their stations, in a bewildered pantomime. The CON-SPIRATORS also appear and consult each other.)*
AUGUSTUS	*(grabbing HECTOR to silence him)* Quiet! Do you want to bring the whole pack down on us?
HECTOR	*(hits AUGUSTUS in the chest; crazed)* Wake up! Wake up! Mother, Father! They're coming for us!

	(HECTOR *tries to run out of the swamp. AUGUSTUS tackles him from behind.*)
AUGUSTUS	Crazy fool! You'll spoil everything! I've. . . come . . . to . . . save you!
	(*A fierce struggle ensues.*)
HECTOR	(*apparently in a vision from his childhood in Africa*)
	Fire! Fire! The huts . . . the boats . . . blood in the water. Run, children, run!
	(*AUGUSTUS gains control and kneels over HECTOR, choking him; HECTOR gasps and is finally still. When AUGUSTUS realizes that HECTOR is dead, he collapses on the lifeless body.*)
AUGUSTUS	Damn you, old man! I came to save you.
	(*After a moment, AUGUSTUS collects himself and stands up, his voice breaking, more pitiful than angry.*)
	Who is not with us, is against us.
HENRY	Selah.
	(*The SLAVES begin humming "Steal Away" as AUGUSTUS kneels and wraps the body in vines, then rolls it under a clump of moss and exposed roots.*)

AUGUSTUS	Let these vines be your shroud, this moss a pillow for your head. These roots will be your coffin, this dark water your grave.
SLAVES	Selah.
AUGUSTUS	Sleep, Hector. Sleep and be free.
	(The SLAVES look at SCYLLA, who lifts her hand slowly.)
SCYLLA	Eshu Elewa ogo gbogbo.
	(BLACKOUT.)

A C T   I I
S C E N E   F I V E

T H E   B I G   H O U S E :
Louis's study; parlor

NARRATOR

Sweet whispers can leave a bitter taste
when a body's supposed to be freedom bound.
Every day as the sun comes easing down,
our man climbs the stairs to sherry and lace.

(Early evening. LOUIS sits hunched over his charts. He is excited.)

LOUIS

Nothing in the books.
Empty sky in all the charts.
And yet I've seen it, with my own eyes!
Last night it was the brightest . . .

(draws a few lines with his compass, looks up wistfully)

What once was a void
fills with feverish matter.

(continues to fiddle with his papers throughout the scene, occasionally jumping up to peer through the telescope)

(AMALIA stands by the fireplace, reading aloud from a book.)

AMALIA

The princess said to her father, "Bring me
strawberries, I am hungry for strawberries."

(shuts the book)

He came back with a husband instead.

(kneels before the fireplace, trying to start it)

"I'm getting too old to tend the garden,"
the king said. "Here is a husband for you—
he will fetch your strawberries."
The princess stomped her foot and replied
if she must have a husband,
she would rather marry the fox,
who at least knew where the sweetest
                                berries grew.
And she ran out of the palace
and into the woods, on and on
until a pebble in her shoe forced her to stop.
But it was not a pebble at all—
it was the king's head, shrunk to the size
of a pea.
"Put me in your pocket,"
the king pleaded, "and take me away
                                with you."
Horrified, the princess threw the king's
                                head down
and ran on. But she had not gone far
before she had to stop again,
and this time when she shook out her shoe,
it was the head of her husband that said:

"Please put me in your pocket
so that I may love you wherever you go."
The princess threw this head down, too,
and ran faster; but before long her shoe
                                    stopped her
for the third time. And this time
it was her own head she held in her hands.

*(She burns her hand, curses softly. There is a
knock at the door. An agitated JONES steps
into the room, leaving the door open.)*

JONES

Beg pardon for the disturbance, Ma'am,
but the matter's urgent.

*(AMALIA rises, pulling her shawl tighter in
exasperation, and takes a seat behind the desk,
glaring.)*

AMALIA

Since you've barged in, Mr. Jones,
the least you can do is close the door.
There's a chill; I believe I've caught it.

JONES

(closes the door, steps up to the desk)

Just what I wanted to talk to you about,
Miss Jennings. This cold spell—
it'll kill the last of the crops
if we don't get them in soon.

(AMALIA doesn't respond.)

JONES (con't.)	Ma'am, you let the niggers leave the fields early.
AMALIA	I thought you'd be happy, Mr. Jones. Aren't such measures part of your economic philosophy?
JONES	Not when there's cotton to be picked.
AMALIA	An hour more or less can hardly matter. Now—this cold spell is unusual, but not as threatening as you make it out to be.
JONES	Well, the niggers sure are spooked. They're just sitting around or looking off in the sky. Matter of fact, they ain't even been tending their own gardens.
AMALIA	This late in the season I don't imagine there's much left to tend.
JONES	And that crazy slave, the one's got the shack out in the swamp—
AMALIA	Hector?
JONES	Yes'm, that's the one I mean. No one's seen hide nor hair of him.
AMALIA	Hector's in the habit of appearing whenever he has snakes to parade.

JONES	But it's been three days, Ma'am!
AMALIA	Cold weather makes the snakes scarce. Is that all, Jones?
JONES	Yes, Ma'am, as you please. Good evening, Miss Jennings.
	(JONES exits, closing the door behind him. AMALIA shakes herself once, briskly, as if trying to restore some measure of reason or calm.)
AMALIA	He's just waiting till the cold clears. He'll be all right.
	(starts toward the window, stops to look in the mirror)
	She looked down at her own head, cradling it in her cupped palms, and cried and cried herself to sleep beneath a giant oak tree. No one heard her. No one came. And so she perished, and her body was never found, even to this day.
	(listening)
	Augustus?
	(AUGUSTUS enters, looking worn and preoccupied. AMALIA runs to embrace him.)

AMALIA	So you've come after all!
	(reaching out to stroke his chest)
	You look tired.
AUGUSTUS	*(uncomfortable)*
	I nearly collided with Jones, barreling full steam across the porch.
AMALIA	Did he see you?
AUGUSTUS	Shadows are kind to niggers.
AMALIA	You're not a nigger!
AUGUSTUS	*(catching her hand by the wrist)*
	Yes I am, Amalia. Best not forget that.
AMALIA	*(leading him to the fire)*
	Come and get warm.
AUGUSTUS	*(hanging back)*
	What did Jones want?
AMALIA	Oh, he was complaining about the weather.
AUGUSTUS	The cold's hard on the crops. They should be picked fast.

AMALIA	*(lightly)*
	Scylla says the weather will break
	<div style="text-align:right">tomorrow.</div>
AUGUSTUS	Since when have you taken to consulting
	<div style="text-align:right">Scylla?</div>
AMALIA	I didn't "consult" her.
	She came up today and said,
	"If it please the Mistress,
	the cold has run its course.
	Morn will break warm, no worry."
AUGUSTUS	Why should you risk your profit
	on Scylla's words?
AMALIA	Look at us, squabbling about agriculture!
	Forget about the weather!
	Who cares what happens out there?
AUGUSTUS	Someone's got to care, Missy.
AMALIA	Don't call me that.
AUGUSTUS	That's what you are. And I'm your slave.
	Nothing has changed that.
AMALIA	*(putting her hand to his mouth; AUGUSTUS withdraws, but only slightly)*
	Shh! If this is all the world they've left us,
	then it's ours to make over.

AMALIA (con't.)	From time to time we can step out to show ourselves to the people so they will have someone to blame.
AUGUSTUS	It's too late.
AMALIA	Don't you think I see the suffering? Don't you think I know I'm the cause?
	(with sarcasm and self-loathing)
	But a master cannot allow himself the privilege of sorrow. A master must rule, or die.
AUGUSTUS	*(pained, thinking of HECTOR)*
	Dying used to be such a simple business. Easy—
	(caresses her neck)
	as long as there was nothing to live for.
	(tightening his grip; AMALIA shows no fear)
	And murder simply a matter of being on the right side of the knife.
AMALIA	*(caressing him, pulling his shirt up)*
	Have you ever used a knife? Have you ever killed someone?

AUGUSTUS	*(haunted, evasive)*
	Now where would I get a knife?
	(turns abruptly away; from outside, barely audible, come the opening strains of "Steal Away")
AMALIA	*(touching each scar on his back as she talks)*
	Your back is like a book no one can bear to read to the end. . . each angry gash, each proud welt. . . But these scars on your side are different.
	(touching them gently)
	They couldn't have come from a whipping. They're more like—more like markings that turn up in fairy tales of princes and paupers exchanged at birth.
AUGUSTUS	I've had them since birth.
AMALIA	So they are magical!
AUGUSTUS	Hardly—unless the art of survival is in your magician's bag of tricks.
	(AMALIA has been caressing him all the while; he begins to return her attentions.)
AMALIA	They even look like crowns. Or suns—exploding suns! How did you come by them?

AUGUSTUS	No more stories.
AMALIA	Please?
AUGUSTUS	Another time. There's enough sorrow on earth tonight. *(embracing her)* And what's the harm in borrowing a little happiness?
AMALIA	Take this, then— *(kisses him)* and this— *(He pulls her down on the sofa as the strains of "Steal Away" grow ever more urgent. AUGUSTUS appears not to hear. He and AMALIA embrace passionately as the light dims.)*

ACT II
SCENE SIX

IN THE SLAVE CEMETERY

(HECTOR's funeral. HECTOR's body is lying in state on a crude platform, covered with a rough blanket. The SLAVES march around the bier as they sing. After a little while JONES enters and stands uncertainly in the background; AMALIA watches from her bedroom window.)

(LOUIS sits at his window but has turned his back. He stares into nothingness, brandy glass in hand.)

SLAVES	Oh Deat' him is a little man, And him goes from do' to do', Him kill some souls and him cripple up, And him lef' some souls to pray. Do Lord, remember me, Do Lord, remember me. I cry to the Lord as de year roll aroun', Lord, remember me.
ALEXANDER	No children, and his kinfolk scattered around this world.
PHEBE	We were all his friends, Alexander.
ALEXANDER	But his youngest child's got to pass over and under! Who's going to do it?

131

PHEBE	Every child on this plantation was like his child, Alexander. Don't you worry.
ALEXANDER	*(breaking down)* To die like that, swoll up and burst open like a—
PHEBE	He's at rest now. He don't feel it. *(The SLAVES stop marching to prepare for the ritual of the "passing." In this rite, the youngest child of the deceased is passed under and over the coffin to signify the continuity of life.)*
SLAVES	My fader's done wid de trouble o' de world, Wid de trouble o' de world, Wid de trouble o' de world, My fader's done wid de trouble o' de world, Outshine de sun. *(AUGUSTUS appears and stands at a distance; PHEBE goes over to him.)*
ALEXANDER	Here he come, stopping by when he's good and ready. Too busy to pay proper respect to the dead.
SCIPIO	Each soul grieves in its own way.
PHEBE	Where were you?

AUGUSTUS	I came soon as I heard—
PHEBE	*(secretive)*
	Not here, man. There.
	(gestures toward the swamp)
	They were calling for you last night. Didn't you hear that "Steal Away?" They sang till I thought the dead would rise out of their graves and follow! I was crazy with worry. Finally I went and told them you couldn't get away.
	(AUGUSTUS glances up at the house, locks gazes with AMALIA.)
	On the way back I tripped over what I thought was an old root, and there he was—
AUGUSTUS	*You* found him?
PHEBE	Under the crook of a mangrove, wrapped in vines. Poor Hector! All those years folks thought he was crazy—
	(looking up at AMALIA's window)
	when he was just sick at heart.

ALEXANDER	Hector took a liking to you, Diana. You should be the one.

(PHEBE joins the mourners as ALEXANDER and SCIPIO pass DIANA under and over the coffin.) |
| SLAVES | Lift him high, Lord, take him by the arm. Wrap him in glory, dip him in balm.

(AUGUSTUS kneels wearily. SCYLLA, ravaged with grief and more stooped than ever, approaches.) |
SCYLLA	He thought evil could be caught.
AUGUSTUS	Yes.
SCYLLA	But evil breeds inside, in the dark. I can smell its sour breath.
AUGUSTUS	Don't come around me, then.
SCYLLA	You believe you can cure the spirit just by riling it. What will these people do with your hate after you free them—as you promise?
AUGUSTUS	I got better things to do than argue with you, Scylla.

SCYLLA	Oh, yes, you're a busy man; you got to watch for people waiting to trip you up; you think danger's on the outside. But do you know what's inside you, Augustus Newcastle? The seeds of the future; they'll have their way. You can't escape. You are in your skin wherever you go. *(turns to the mourners, who have just completed the ritual of the passing, and calls out)* Eshu Elewa ogo gbogbo!
ALEXANDER	He's gone over. He's flown on the wind.
SCYLLA	He came with no mother to soothe him. He came with no father to teach him. He came with no names for his gods.
PHEBE	No way but to see it through.
SCYLLA	Who can I talk to about his journey? He stood tall, so they bent his back. He found love, so they ate his heart. Eshu Elewa ogo gbogbo!
SCIPIO	This is what a man comes to.
SCYLLA	Who will remember him, without a father, without a mother?

PHEBE	Poor people, you've lost your wings.
SCYLLA	Eshu Elewa ogo gbogbo! Where are the old words now? Scattered by the wind.
ALEXANDER	The body a feather, the spirit a flame.
SCYLLA	And now the sun has come out to warm him.
SCIPIO	Too late! He's flown.
SCYLLA	But the wind won't carry me!
	(The SLAVES hum and chant as they disperse, their song becoming gradually less mournful and more urgent as we segue into the next scene.)
NARRATOR	Sunday evening; New moon, skies clear. The wheel's stopped turning: Redemption's here.

136

ACT II
SCENE SEVEN

NEAR THE SLAVE CABINS

(Early evening, shortly before sunset: PHEBE and AUGUSTUS come from the shadows. In the background the SLAVES go about evening chores while singing, a mixture of militant spirituals and African chants, with whispered phrases such as "Rise up!" or "Mean to be free!" occasionally audible.)

AUGUSTUS	Everything's ready.
PHEBE	Yes.
AUGUSTUS	We've been careful.
PHEBE	Oh, yes.
AUGUSTUS	*(pacing)* Any day now. Any time!
PHEBE	It's been three days, Augustus— three days since you heard the call and didn't answer.
AUGUSTUS	Tonight's new moon; skies are clear. Destiny calls!
PHEBE	Are you sure it's not just your destiny?
AUGUSTUS	What do you mean?

PHEBE	Every time you talk about victory and vengeance, it's as if you're saying my victory, my vengeance. As if you didn't care about anyone's pain but yours.
AUGUSTUS	Are you with us, or against us?
PHEBE	Ain't nothing wrong with feelings, Augustus—just where they lead you. Now when it comes to hating, you and Miss Amalia are a lot alike.

(AUGUSTUS whirls, but she stands her ground.)

She used to be different—high-minded,
but always ready to laugh.
When she married Massa Louis
she began to sour.
Seemed like disappointment killed her.

(hesitates, then hurries through)

And now you've brought her back to life.
No wonder you're mixed up!

AUGUSTUS	Why are you telling me this?
PHEBE	Because I care what happens to you more than revolution or freedom. Those may be traitor's words, but

I don't care. 'Cause maybe—
maybe if you hadn't let hate
take over your life, you might have
had some love left over for me.

(*She runs off. AUGUSTUS slowly sits down,
as if a new and treacherous path had opened
before him. BENJAMIN and HENRY enter unseen.
AUGUSTUS buries his face in his hands.*)

BENJAMIN

(*whispering*)

There he is. Don't look
so fearful now, does he?

(*makes a bird call*)

AUGUSTUS   Who's there?

(*He leaps to his feet; the CONSPIRATORS
approach.*)

BENJAMIN   May Fate be with you.

AUGUSTUS   You've brought news?

BENJAMIN   Most of the news is old, brother.

AUGUSTUS   It couldn't be helped;
I was under constant guard.

BENJAMIN   Constant guard? Constant companionship
would be closer to the truth.

AUGUSTUS	Talk straight!
BENJAMIN	Straight as a bullet, brother. You sent word that you were "being watched"— Naturally, we sent someone to see about your difficulties. What a surprise to find out who your guard was and how tenderly she watched over you!
AUGUSTUS	Missy needed a buck—what of it?
BENJAMIN	Sound mighty proud, buck.
AUGUSTUS	Just the facts, brother, just the facts. Should I knock her hand away to prove my loyalty to the cause? Why not charm her instead?
BENJAMIN	That never used to be your style.
AUGUSTUS	I've never been so close to freedom.
BENJAMIN	All the more reason to see you don't spoil it. *(looks skyward)* The night's perfect: clear skies, new moon.
AUGUSTUS	Tonight? I knew it! I'll assemble my forces.

BENJAMIN	Hold on. You'll be coming with us.
AUGUSTUS	But—
BENJAMIN	You told us what you wanted us to believe. We've got orders to bring you to headquarters. They'll decide what's to be done.
AUGUSTUS	I can't leave. My people need me!
BENJAMIN	This is death's business, brother. Even a nigger as famous as you can't be given the benefit of the doubt! Your second-in-command will organize things here.
AUGUSTUS	Phebe?
	(BENJAMIN takes AUGUSTUS by the arm.)
BENJAMIN	Henry will deliver her orders. We'll wait in the wagon. Come on!
	(All exit; BLACKOUT. The chanting of the SLAVES grows louder, with snatches of spirituals in high descant, but the lyrics are volatile. The percussive, more African-based chants prevail, with key phrases like "Freedom, children, freedom!" emerging ever stronger through the next scene.)

A C T I I
S C E N E E I G H T

T H E B I G H O U S E :
Amalia's bedroom, Louis's study, hallway

(Evening: LOUIS stands at the open window of his study, looking through the telescope, alternately at the night sky and down over the plantation grounds.)

(AMALIA sits on the window seat in her bedroom. PHEBE enters.)

PHEBE	You wanted me, Ma'am?
AMALIA	Good evening, Phebe! I was sitting at the window, catching the last rays of sunlight, when I happened to see you darting from group to group, talking to this slave and that, and I said to myself: "Perhaps Phebe would like to talk to me, too."
PHEBE	*(on her guard)* I'm pleased to talk conversation whenever you like, Miss Amalia.
AMALIA	*(slightly sarcastic)*

It seems you're mighty pleased
with other people's conversations
these days.

PHEBE   I don't follow your meaning, Ma'am.

AMALIA   Oh, really? I notice
             you and Augustus have no problem
             following each other's meaning.

PHEBE   Augustus ain't nothing
             but a friend, Ma'am.
             I don't recollect talking to him
             any more than anyone else.

             (laughs nervously)

             Me and my big mouth always be
             yakking at somebody or another.

AMALIA   Don't talk yourself
             into trouble, Phebe.

PHEBE   Beg pardon, Ma'am.
             I didn't mean nothing by it.

AMALIA   Everyone can see
             you're making a fool of yourself
             over him! Have you spoken
             to Augustus today?

PHEBE   I can't rightly say, Ma'am.

PHEBE (con't.)	*(at a warning look from AMALIA)*
	That is—I talked to a lot of people and he was amongst them, but we didn't say more than a how-de-do.
AMALIA	Tell Augustus I want to see him.
PHEBE	*(thrown into panic)*
	I don't know—I mean—
AMALIA	What's the matter, Phebe?
PHEBE	Nothing, Ma'am. It might take a while, is all.
AMALIA	*(sarcastic)*
	And why is that?
PHEBE	It's just—well, Augustus been keeping to himself lately. I seen him going off in the direction of the swamp; he's got some crazy idea about fixing up Hector's shack.
AMALIA	*(haunted)*
	Oh. When he returns, send him up.
PHEBE	Yes, Ma'am.

(PHEBE *exits. In the hallway she runs into* AUGUSTUS. *He is very agitated.*)

PHEBE

(whispering)

You! Here?

AUGUSTUS

Yes. They sent me back.

PHEBE

I thought for sure they was going to do
something awful to you.

AUGUSTUS

The sun travels its appointed track,
a knot of fire, day in day out—
what could be more awful?

PHEBE

Augustus, what is it?
Can I help?

AUGUSTUS

This job I do alone.

PHEBE

But surely you can take a minute
to go in there and smooth
that she-hawk's feathers down
so's the rest of us can—

(AMALIA *steps out and peers into the dim hall.* AUGUSTUS *shrinks into the shadows.*)

AMALIA

Is that you, Phebe?

PHEBE

Yes'm. I was just on my way downstairs.

AMALIA	I heard voices.
PHEBE	That was me, Ma'am. I twisted my foot in the dark— guess I was talking to it. *(laughs nervously)* My mama used to say it helps to talk the hurt out.
AMALIA	Well, do your talking elsewhere. Go on! *(PHEBE hesitates, then exits. AMALIA stands looking into the darkness for a moment, then goes back into her room. AUGUSTUS steps out of hiding, holding a knife.)*
AUGUSTUS	"Prove you haven't betrayed the cause! Kill them both—your mistress and her foolish husband." That's Fate for you, Amalia. *(looks at the knife)* That white throat, bared for kisses . . . one quick pass, and it will flow redder than a thousand roses. Everything was so simple before! Hate and be hated. But this—love or freedom— is the devil's choice.

(*Steeling himself, he heads for LOUIS's room. Lights up on LOUIS, who is sitting with his right hand tucked nervously in the lap of his dressing gown. His back is to AUGUSTUS, who enters stealthily.*)

LOUIS

(*startling AUGUSTUS, who stops in his tracks*)

No one has come through that door
for years. You're the new one, aren't you?

(*pulls a pistol out of his lap*)

A wild nigger, I hear. Amalia's latest
                                    indulgence.

AUGUSTUS

So this is the great white master,
trembling in his dressing gown!

LOUIS

Beware of the Moon in the house of Mars!

(*stands up and turns, hiding the pistol as he and AUGUSTUS face off*)

The stars can tell you everything—
war and pestilence, love and betrayal.

AUGUSTUS

War? Yes, this is war. Say your prayers,
Massa—you have a hard ride ahead of you.

LOUIS

A hard ride, me? I don't think so.

(*aims his pistol at AUGUSTUS*)

LOUIS (con't.)	A man should be able to kill when he has to, don't you agree? *(Startled by this unexpected turn of events, AUGUSTUS freezes. LOUIS reaches for the bottle on the table with his other hand.)* Perhaps you'd care for a bit of bourbon to warm your way?
AUGUSTUS	*(trying to compose himself)* You can't stop what's coming over the hill.
LOUIS	*(shakes his pistol at Augustus, shouting)* This time I won't leave things up to chance! *(muttering)* What a fool I was! I should have smothered the bastard right there in the basket. That's the man's way.
AUGUSTUS	Basket? What basket?
LOUIS	Amalia's, of course. Amalia's basket. It was— *(slight pause; distracted)*

The doctor refused to kill it.
What else was there to do?

(*AUGUSTUS lunges, knocking the gun from LOUIS's hand and overpowering him.*)

AUGUSTUS   There goes your last chance, fool!

(*drags LOUIS by the collar toward center stage*)

This basket—what did it look like?

LOUIS   What do you care?

AUGUSTUS   (*holds the knife to LOUIS's throat*)

Enough to slit your throat.

LOUIS   (*whimpering*)

Oh, it was beautiful! White wicker,
lined in blue satin, tiny red rosettes
marching along the rim . . .

AUGUSTUS   (*slowly lets go of LOUIS's collar*)

And your spurs slipped right inside.

LOUIS   Amalia's Christmas present.
Oh, was the good doctor relieved!
"It's a miracle," he said,
"but the child's still alive!"

AUGUSTUS	And still lives to this day. Spurs bite into a horse's belly— think what they can do to a newborn child! *(rips open his shirt)*
LOUIS	You?
AUGUSTUS	All my life I tried to imagine what you would look like. Would you be tall or stooped over? Blue eyes, or brown? Would you dress in white linen or dash around in a dusty greatcoat? To think that your blood flows through my veins— *(advances on LOUIS, who staggers back into the chair)*
LOUIS	My blood?
AUGUSTUS	When I think of you forcing your wretched seed into my mother, I want to rip you—
LOUIS	Me, your father? You think I'm your father?
AUGUSTUS	I heard it from your own lips.

LOUIS	*(bursts into laughter)*
	Of course! Of course!
	The stars said it all:
	Who is born into violence
	shall live to fulfill it.
	Who shuns violence
	will die by the sword.
AUGUSTUS	*(pulls LOUIS from the chair, knife at his throat)*
	What happened to my mother?
	What did you do to her?
LOUIS	*(in a crafty voice)*
	I haven't touched her since.
	Ask Amalia—
	she runs this plantation.
	She knows your mother better than anyone!
AUGUSTUS	Amalia? Of course!
	Missy wanted the bastard child dead.
	Now I understand: It's an old story.
LOUIS	You understand nothing.
	(A sudden shout outside; the revolt has begun. Both men freeze, listening.)
AUGUSTUS	It's time!
	(stabs LOUIS as the sounds of the revolt grow)

LOUIS	You were there. . . all along. . .
AUGUSTUS	*(letting LOUIS's body drop)*
	So, Amalia—and to think I tried to bargain for your life!
SLAVES	Freedom! Freedom! Selah! Selah!
	(AUGUSTUS heads for AMALIA's room; lights come up on AMALIA, who has stepped into the hall.)
AMALIA	Augustus, there you are! What's happening? I called Ticey, but she won't come!
AUGUSTUS	*(backing her into the room)*
	I thought you didn't care what happened out there.
AMALIA	Why are they shouting? Why doesn't Jones make them stop?
AUGUSTUS	I reckon the dead don't make good overseers. Your slaves are rebelling, Missy. Liberté, Égalité, Fraternité!
AMALIA	*(stares at him uncomprehendingly, then runs to the window)*

Rebelling? My slaves?
Augustus, make them stop!
They'll listen to you!

AUGUSTUS   Like I listened to you?
                You led me into your parlor
                like a dog on a leash. Sit, dog!
                Heel! Care for a sherry? A fairy tale?

AMALIA   No, you were different!
                You were—

AUGUSTUS   (grabs her)

                No more conversation!
                Where is my mother?

AMALIA   Your mother? How would I know
                                    a thing like that?

AUGUSTUS   Your husband confessed!

AMALIA   (aware of danger on all sides, seeking escape)

                What could Louis have to confess?

AUGUSTUS   A shrewd piece of planning,
                to destroy him with his own son
                after you had failed to destroy
                the son himself!
                But you had to be patient.
                Twenty years you had to wait
                before you could buy me back.

AMALIA	Louis, your father? You must be joking!
AUGUSTUS	Shall I help you remember? You supplied the basket yourself—
AMALIA	Basket?
AUGUSTUS	—lined in blue satin, trimmed with rosettes—
AMALIA	*Red* rosettes?
AUGUSTUS	Monsieur LaFarge agreed to sell his own baby—but that wasn't enough, was it? You wanted the child dead. So you slipped a pair of riding spurs into the sewing basket. And you know the kind of scars spurs leave, Missy. Like crowns. . . or exploding suns.
AMALIA	My God.
AUGUSTUS	The woman who patched me up kept that basket as a reminder.
AMALIA	No. . .
AUGUSTUS	*(shakes her)* Who is my mother? What did you do with her? *(slaps her)* Tell me!

AMALIA	*(wrenches free to face him; her voice trembling)*
	So you want to know who your mother is?
	You think, if I tell you,
	the sad tale of your life
	will find its storybook ending?
	Well then, this will be my last story—
	and when I have finished,
	you will wish you had never
	stroked my hair or kissed my mouth.
	You will wish you had no eyes to see
	or ears to hear. You will wish
	you had never been born.
AUGUSTUS	I've heard grown men scream,
	watched as the branding iron
	sank into their flesh. I've seen
	pregnant women slit open like melon,
	runaways staked to the ground and
	whipped until
	they floated in their own blood and piss.
	Don't think you can frighten me, Missy:
	Nothing your lips can tell
	can be worse than what
	these eyes have seen.
AMALIA	Bravo! What a speech!
	But you've seen nothing.
	(backs up to appraise him, smiling, slightly delirious)

155

AMALIA (con't.)	That same expression! How could I forget? My lover then stood as tall as you now.
AUGUSTUS	Your lover?
	(PHEBE bursts in.)
PHEBE	They're coming, Augustus! They're coming to see if you did what you were told! Oh Augustus— you were supposed to kill her!
AUGUSTUS	*(shaking himself into action, threatening AMALIA)* My mother, who is my mother? Out with it!
AMALIA	Phebe, you tell him. You were there. Everyone was there— under my window, waiting for news . . .
PHEBE	That . . . was the night we all came to wait out the birth.
AUGUSTUS	What birth?
AMALIA	Hector on the porch.
AUGUSTUS	What about Hector?

	(More shouts outside; compelled by the urgency of the growing revolution, PHEBE tries to distract AUGUSTUS.)
PHEBE	There's no time!
AUGUSTUS	*(grabs AMALIA as if to slit her throat)* What about Hector?
AMALIA	Chick in a basket, going to market! They said you died, poor thing. That's why Hector went to the swamp. *(AUGUSTUS stares desperately at her. PHEBE turns, thunderstruck.)*
AUGUSTUS	Hector?
AMALIA	But you didn't die. You're here. . . *(reaches for him; he draws back)*
PHEBE	*(looks from AMALIA to AUGUSTUS, horror growing; recites tonelessly)* Stepped on a pin, the pin bent, and that's the way the story went.
AMALIA	*(sadly, in a small voice)* Silk for my prince, and a canopy of roses! You were so tiny . . . so sweet and tiny. I didn't know about the spurs.

PHEBE

You sold your own child.
Hector's child.

AUGUSTUS

Hector . . .

(The knife slips from his fingers.)

AMALIA

I was trying to save you!

AUGUSTUS

Save me?

AMALIA

(extremely agitated)

I felt like they had hacked out my heart.
But I wouldn't let them see me cry.

AUGUSTUS

(wrestling with the horror)

You? My mother?

AMALIA

(clutching herself)

It was like missing an arm or a leg
that pains and throbs, even though
you can look right where it was
and see there's nothing left.

(She stops abruptly.)

AUGUSTUS

My own mother gave me away.
But I found my way back . . .
a worm crawling into its hole.

AMALIA	For weeks afterwards my breasts ached with milk.
AUGUSTUS	*(sinking to his knees)* Better I had bled to death in that basket. *(A great shout goes up as the insurrectionists gain entry to the main house. AMALIA takes advantage of the ensuing distraction to pick up the knife.)*
PHEBE	Augustus!
AUGUSTUS	*(passive)* The Day of Redemption is here.
PHEBE	They'll kill you, Augustus!
AUGUSTUS	Time to be free.
AMALIA	Poor baby! I thought I could keep you from harm— and here you are, right in harm's way. *(PHEBE gasps; AMALIA stabs herself as AUGUSTUS, alerted by PHEBE's gasp, jumps up, too late to stop her. The room turns red as the outbuildings go up in flames.)*

AUGUSTUS	Amalia!
	(catching her as she falls)
	No. . .
	(calling out in anguish)
	Eshu Elewa ogo gbogbo!
	(The chanting of the rebelling SLAVES grows louder.)
PHEBE	Oh, Augustus . . .
AUGUSTUS	*(lays AMALIA's body down, gently)*
	I had the sun and the moon once. And the stars with their cool gaze. Now it's dark.
PHEBE	It's all right. You'll be all right now.
AUGUSTUS	*(staring as if trying to make out something in the distance)*
	Who's there? How she stares, like a cat at midnight!
PHEBE	Nobody's there, Augustus.

AUGUSTUS	Don't you see her?
	(PHEBE shakes her head, terrified.)
	Look, she's hidden behind a tree.
PHEBE	Oh, Augus—

AUGUSTUS	Shh! You'll frighten her. There's another one—
	he's been flogged and pickled in brine.
	That skinny boy ate dirt; that's why he
	          staggers.
	So many of them, limping, with brands
	          on their cheeks!
	Oh, I can't bear it!

PHEBE	Come along, now.
AUGUSTUS	*(calling out to the "ghosts")*
	I came to save you!
	(The SLAVES burst in, brandishing bayonets and torches.)
BENJAMIN	He did it.
SLAVES	Selah! We're free!
	(The slaves lift AUGUSTUS onto their shoulders. The SLAVE WOMAN/NARRATOR stands at the door, holding a torch, taking in the scene.)
SLAVES	Freedom, freedom, freedom . . .

(The "Freedom!" chant grows louder and more persistent as the slaves parade out of the room, AUGUSTUS on their shoulders; PHEBE follows them, sobbing. SCYLLA takes the torch from the SLAVE WOMAN/ NARRATOR and sets fire to the window's billowing curtains as she slowly straightens up to her full height.)

(BLACKOUT.)

THE END

THE AUTHOR

Rita Dove served as Poet Laureate of the United States and Consultant in Poetry at the Library of Congress from 1993 to 1995. Born in 1952 in Akron, Ohio and a 1970 Presidential Scholar as one of the top hundred U.S. high school graduates that year, she majored in English at Miami University of Ohio, studied German and European literatures as a Fulbright scholar at Universität Tübingen in Germany, and received her master of fine arts in creative writing from the University of Iowa in 1977. She has since published six poetry collections, among them *Thomas and Beulah*, which was awarded the Pulitzer Prize in 1987, and most recently *Mother Love*. She is also the author of a book of short stories and the novel *Through the Ivory Gate*. In 1995 the Library of Congress published her laureate lectures under the title *The Poet's World*. *The Darker Face of the Earth* is her first full-length play, premiering at the Oregon Shakespeare Festival in the summer of 1996.

Rita Dove's literary and academic honors include Guggenheim and Mellon fellowships, grants from the National Endowment for the Arts and the National Endowment for the Humanities, as well as residencies at Tuskegee Institute, the National Humanities Center and the Rockefeller Foundation's Villa Serbelloni in Bellagio, Italy. Ms. Dove is also the recipient of the Academy of American Poets' Lavan Award, a General Electric Foundation Award, the New York Public Library's Literary Lion medal, the NAACP Great American Artist Award, a Golden Plate Award from the American Academy of Achievement, the Folger Shakespeare Library's Renaissance Forum Award for leadership in the literary arts, *Glamour* magazine's "Women of the Year" Award, twelve honorary doctorates, and many other recognitions.

Rita Dove is Commonwealth Professor of English at the University of Virginia in Charlottesville, where she lives with her husband and daughter.